Jackie Woodside has done an amazing job of presenting valuable information that can positively change the way you experience time in your life! She brings clarity and a practical plan to a world that is getting faster and more chaotic by the minute. *Calming The Chaos* is a great guide to mastering the elusive nature of "time" by putting you in both action and trust with the flow of life. This book is highly recommended to anyone looking to experience more peace and realize more time when there seems to be none!

Howard Falco
Spiritual Teacher and Author of *Time in a Bottle: Mastering The Experience of Life* and *I AM: The Power of Discovering Who You Really Are*

From ending procrastination to scheduling priorities, Jackie has all sorts of practical suggestions for getting more done and feeling better about it. She knows that 'I'm too busy' is just an excuse that keeps us from living the lives we want.

Laura Vanderkam
Author, *Their Own Sweet Time (2015), 168 Hours*, and *What the Most Successful People Do Before Breakfast* -- a paperback compilation of the bestselling ebook series, all from Portfolio/Penguin. Please visit www.lauravanderkam.com.

Jackie is a new and powerful voice in the field of consciousness evolution. Her book, *Calming the Chaos*, is a practical and an excellent resource for those who want to increase their awareness along with their productivity.

Bruce D Schneider
Founder, Institute for Professional Excellence in Coaching (iPEC)
and author of *Energy Leadership*

Jackie's approach is both practical and profound. Leaders and people from all backgrounds can benefit from this clear and thoughtful framework to access their boundless inner resources to navigate everyday life. Learning to manage your Self in time is key in the creation of a happy, effective, and balanced way of life. *Calming the Chaos* provides an inspiring and practical roadmap for making our most mundane tasks spiritually uplifting and a service to others.

Zayda Vallejo, M.Litt.
Founder of The HeartWell Institute for Mindful Living, adjunct faculty at the Center for Mindfulness in Medicine, Health Care and Society at the University of Massachusetts Medical School, instructor at the Department of Psychiatry in the School of Medicine at the University of Massachusetts, Worcester

There are many great teachers in this world, but few can — practically and with clarity — teach life. Jackie's *Calming The Chaos* gives us, in sensible, down to earth, language how to actively apply a profound concept. It really is about Energetic Consciousness! This is, seriously, a must-read.

Rob McGrath
Principal at Wind Rose Retreats
Stratton, Vermont

At a time when so many people are immersed in feeling C.H.A.O.S. (Confused, Hurried, Agitated, Overwhelmed, and Scared), Jackie Woodside's *Calming the Chaos* offers an amazing and timely dose of soulful and practical ways to realign us to our purpose, passion, and point of focus so that we may travel toward our True North! Jackie, has outlined in very clear and applicable ways that we can identify those blockages and hindrances to living the lives we deserve and once identified, she helps us to remove them and then access an energy we may not have realized was ours to tap into! I give the book 10 out of 5 stars!

Rev. Dr. Raymont L. Anderson, Ph.D
Speaker, author, seminar leader

Calming the Chaos helps to de-mystify what conscious awareness is really all about. In so doing Jackie offers very practical insights into the power of choice, living in the present, projecting one's own positive energy and ultimately taking control of your life. You are ready for action once you read this book."

Bill Sex
President, New England Coaching

I really like how Jackie provides a practical approach to calming the chaos. Her use of examples taken from her own life experience helped illuminate the points she made in the book. I have some great takeaways to help me manage my energy.

Terry Durkin, MBA, EA
Owner, Durkin Associates

CALMING
THE
CHAOS

CALMING
— THE —
CHAOS

*A Soulful Guide to Managing Your Energy
Rather Than Your Time*

JACKIE WOODSIDE
CPC, LICSW

NEXT CENTURY
PUBLISHING

Calming the Chaos: A Soulful Guide for Managing Your Energy
Rather Than Your Time

Published by Next Century Publishing
www.NextCenturyPublishing.com
Las Vegas, NV

ISBN: 978-1-62903-822-3

Library of Congress Control Number: 2014960107

Printed in the United States of America

Dedication

For Heather

Acknowledgements

As with any project of significance or importance, there is a wonderful group of people who have supported, cheered, helped, guided and mentored me along the way. I hope to capture my sentiments to all of you here.

To my team at Next Century Publishing: Ken, Simon, Shannon, Margo, Morpheus, Jason and Rod–I cannot thank you enough for your ongoing encouragement and belief not only in my message, but also in me as a messenger. Your confidence and enthusiasm bolstered my stamina when I thought I could not get this done. Thank you for your excellence in the work that you do. To my impeccably skilled proofreader, Maria Alma Nevedo, you are such a blessing in my life. Thank you for your unrelenting commitment to my work!

To my core group of students: especially those of you who were early graduates of my Curriculum for Conscious Living–Patty Barkas, Char Carver, Ruth Cook, Rose Couzzo, Jane Cowan, Arlene Dorischild, Amy Joslin, Nancy Langmeyer, Steve Hermann, Catherine Ives, Cherlyn Kast, Thea Klein, Martha McCown, Jan Goddard Taylor, Mary Rapa, Gary Taylor and Bev Wedda – your resilience and commitment to living a transformed life continue to call me higher. And posthumously, to Nancy Lincoln, who through her courage, acceptance and grace taught us how to live a transcendent life, even unto death. I cannot thank you enough–there are no words to convey the depth at which your belief in me, your faith in my mission and your willingness to keep showing up and doing this work has helped to create this dream. You are my students, my fellow journeyers and my friends.

As always, deep gratitude and love to my family, with whom I savor each day in this delicious life we are co-creating!

My constant commitment is to make my life a living prayer–to live and fulfill my mission in everything that I do. May this book serve that end for each and every one of you.

CALMING

— THE —

CHAOS

Table of Contents

Introduction

I meet with hundreds of people every year to talk about this notion of time, chaos and overwhelm. I repeatedly hear difficult, challenging and painful emotions that emerge in discussing this ephemeral resource. We have such an odd and unrealistic relationship with time, giving it otherworldly power and characteristics that we allow to deeply impact the quality of our lives. We relate to time both as a blessing and a curse, depending on what is happening around us. We lament its passing. We scoff at its scarcity. I have worked with prison inmates who wanted time to pass more quickly and who felt that all they had was time, and I have worked with those facing terminal illness who desperately wanted more of this precious, yet unseen raw material.

As human beings we have the ability to reflect on and alter our perceptions. It requires a certain level of self-awareness and maturity, but we have the capacity to wake up and live more consciously. Yet, as you may have noticed, we have a strong inclination to stay asleep, lulled into unconsciousness by habits and proclivities and the non-stop stimulation in the world around us. Each day, each moment in fact, we have the option of moving forward with greater clarity and power, or to remain in the same state of chaos and despair.

We long for greater freedom and peace –to feel more calm, less stressed and frantic– and who can blame us? But the challenge comes when we are asked to look deeply at ourselves, at our habits and perceptions and begin the often arduous task of unlearning long-held beliefs and undoing long-established behaviors in service of something higher. A higher order, an easier way is possible, but it will not occur through the methods and means available to us in mainstream culture. It is not going to come from doing things faster, more efficiently or more right-sized. It will come when you begin staking claim in the ownership and authority of your own life–which means transforming your relationship to time.

The flow of this book follows the process necessary to create change in any and every area of life. We'll start with your self-awareness, because you have to find the "You Are Here" dot on a map before you can make your way forward. Becoming *aware* of your own unique contribution to the chaos in your life is the primary place to go to work, because you cannot change what you cannot or are unwilling to see. You must begin by taking stock of how your current consciousness, habits, beliefs and ways of being form a powerful foundation for the rest of your journey toward calming the chaos.

As a speaker, trainer, therapist, consultant and coach, I talk with a lot of people about this notion of awareness. It is an elusive quality that can feel a little bit like walking in a labyrinth with the ever-present question, "Am I there yet?" How aware is aware enough? Far too often people profess owning a high degree of self-awareness, but then when I listen to them, what I hear is their keen awareness of the "other" rather than the self: the other person who is slighting them, the situation that is causing angst, the myriad reasons for their lot in life being what it is. None of this is what I consider to be true self-awareness.

I define self-awareness as the ability to consistently observe and alter your feelings (emotion), reactions (behavior), and level of consciousness (being) in regard to any circumstance at any given time. Self-awareness observes how YOU are thinking, feeling and responding, as well as observes the responses and events around you. To take this one step further, self-awareness is also not "I am upset *because you did or said X thing to me.*" Self-awareness says, "I am upset. What am I making this situation mean such that I would respond with feeling upset? What am I attached to having gone my way? Where am I feeling superior or slighted such that my feelings got hurt?" These are questions that look within for the source of difficulty rather than look at the external conditions in one's life. There is far too little of this inquiry in our Tweet-a-thought, 140-character world.

You will have the opportunity to think about how you schedule yourself in relation to time as you get into the section of this book on Self-Management. You will learn the ways you are often unconscious about time and how this unconsciousness leads to the buildup of stress when you do not locate what you are doing in a solid notion of time.

The "Skills and Practices" section will give you the actual techniques to begin to effect change. These are things as simple as throwing away your clutter and as complicated as restructuring your relationships. What needs to take place is different for everyone, but it's as transformative as it is practical.

The final step of *Calming the Chaos* is turning what you've learned into habits. This isn't a temporary diet you take on for a month in order to lose a few pounds before your daughter's wedding. This is a new way of living and being, and it has to be maintained in order to work. I'll show you how to do that.

I write this book from years of real-life experience, my own and thousands of others who have used these methods. But most of all, I want you to know that this book has been a remedy for what ails me. Long ago diagnosed with Adult Attention Deficit Disorder, I have used these methods to help calm my own chaos, set my direction in life and bring peace and productivity to my days. By consistently applying these techniques and philosophies, I have stopped using the pharmaceuticals that helped focus my brain (Oh, how I miss them sometimes!!). But I did not want to live my life being chemically stimulated to focus my mind and direct my soul. I knew, I believed, I trusted that there was another way. The work in this book came to me when I was on Cape Cod in a silent retreat asking for the direction and guidance I needed to elevate my life. Whether or not you believe in a deity that has a hand in the workings of our lives, I truly feel like I was given this material to share, in hope of calming the chaos for millions of others who are perhaps very similar to me.

I call living with an attention deficit condition the blessing and the curse of being a high-creativity, high-intelligence and high-consciousness person! To people like us, it is a *big world out there,* and all of it is interesting! Without any inner regulator that guides and directs our energy, we may well be left to follow one bright idea after another, yet accomplishing very little.

The principles in this book ended my cycle of nonstop activity and chaos, and it is my hope that it will serve that same purpose for you. On the other side of chaos lie fulfillment, satisfaction and peace of mind. They are there for you to discover and create.

* Author's note: While I have used stories of various clients throughout this book, each person's name and identifying information have been altered to protect the identity of the client. All stories have been used with permission.

Section One: A New Paradigm

Things are not happening to you, they are happening for you.

~Howard Falco, author of "Time in a Bottle"

Chapter One

Debunking the Myth of Time and Stress Management

The science of stamina has advanced to the point where individuals, teams, and whole organizations can, with some straightforward interventions, significantly increase their capacity to get things done.

~Tony Schwartz, Business consultant, author

I just finished a group coaching call where I was working with the concepts in this book. During the call, one of the participants made a statement that bolstered my resolve to get this book out. "This work is revolutionary, truly life-changing." And she is right. What is different about *Calming the Chaos* is that it debunks so much of the prevailing mindset about how our culture is living in relation to time, being overwhelmed and getting things done.

There is something about the way we are living and moving and being in life that just doesn't seem to be working. What I am talking about is the constant sense of frenzy, chaos and overwhelm that so many people in our culture live in, similar to wearing their favorite old, worn-out sweater. But how do we shed something that has become so familiar, that lends a sense of permanence and importance to our very lives?

Everyone is busy, so busy, too busy, crazy busy. It matters little if I am speaking to my 77-year-old retired mother or my minister or the teenager who babysits my son; everyone everywhere is moving through life at warp speed, searching for something, that one thing that may be the elixir to what ails us. Yet what ails us, for the most part, does not relate to what is happening around us, but rather what is happening *within* us.

So much of what you think about and talk about has to do with what you are managing in life. There is so much for us to manage! We manage our time, our weight, our stress, our finances, our social media accounts, the stock market, the inflow of media and our work/life balance. In fact, we are managing so much that the managing of life has taken on a life of its own! It is what I call surviving rather than thriving.

Instead of trying (often fruitlessly) to manage all of these disparate parts of our lives, perhaps there needs to be a new focus. Rather than focusing "out there" on the externals, the stuff, the doingness of life, perhaps there is a new way of seeing. A revolution is at hand, and it is one in which our inner world becomes the primary determinant of how to experience life, rather than what we own, have, produce and yes, rather than what we manage.

Rather than trying to manage time and stress and productivity, perhaps all we need to do is learn to manage our energy and ourselves. What a revolution this would bring! Time management? No more! Stress management? No longer an issue! Why? Because we have learned, once and for all, that managing time, which is a finite resource, simply does not work. Managing energy, on the other hand, is a whole new frontier. As Tony Schwartz and Catherine McCarthy write in *Manage Your Energy, Not Your Time,*"... energy can be systematically expanded and regularly renewed by establishing specific rituals–behaviors that are intentionally practiced and precisely scheduled, with the goal of making them unconscious and automatic as quickly as possible." (Harvard Business Review, 2010).

Calming the Chaos addresses the immense challenge, honor, and blessing of living life in the 21st century as awake, aware, educated, capable, intelligent and curious people who are engaged in life. The paradox of our society is the enormous richness and variety of our cultural offerings and experiences. We have access to so much of life's "good stuff" that such expansive access creates a conundrum of sorts. There is so much that we *can* do, see, touch, taste, learn, explore and experience, that when we move nonstop from one thing to the next, in essence we truly experience very little of it. What ends up missing is not time to *do* more, but time to *feel* more–to integrate more, to process and absorb more. What is missing is meaningful time.

The truth is that when you say "Yes!" to everything, you are really saying "No" to your peace of mind. That is what we are grappling with in contemporary culture, and it requires a skill set and way of being in the world that are radically different from how we currently live.

Calming the Chaos means *doing things differently* (i.e. learning new skills) and *being different in the world* (i.e. thinking and perceiving things in a new way). The doing domain is what I call "content" while the being domain is the "context" of your life. We live at intersection of these two domains. Having one without the other only perpetuates what isn't working about the way we are living. Having a new, higher perception of time, your choices and actions without having wildly different skills for managing yourself and your life will leave you ineffective at creating the outcomes you desire. Yet, having wildly better skills without a changed perception of time will leave you forever chasing the next great thing "out there" that leaves you once again empty and dissatisfied.

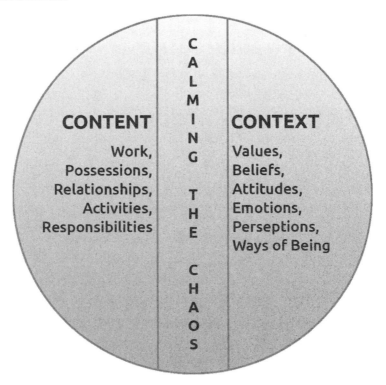

This may sound like a lofty and intangible goal, but as human beings we have the capacity to raise our awareness and alter our habits of thinking and behaving. When we do so, we can make different, better and higher choices. Choices that empower us, rather than drag us down or keep us frantically trapped in the chaos of our contemporary world. While we have the capacity for greater awareness, what is too often the case is that we remain asleep; numbed in a frenzy of activity and busyness that drains our very soul.

What is different about this approach is that it recognizes the fact there is no such thing as "managing time." Time is a resource, a commodity that we all have the same access to. How can we control *time* when it moves of its own accord? The sun creeps through the sky as we spin on our earth's axis; the tides push and pull with the moon; seconds tick by, one after another, each the same as the last, whether we want them to or not.

I won't ever be able to find more than twenty-four hours in a day and I promise you, neither will you. Whether you are working full time, running multiple businesses, staying at home raising children, or retired, you and I have the same resource in front of us. We all have the same 24/7, so TIME is not the variable. *The variable is your ability to manage yourself in relation to time.*

For most people, that is good news and bad news. Many of the people I work with walk around feeling there is something wrong with them—they just can't keep up the way other people seem to. They feel they must be fundamentally deficient in managing time, or prioritizing better, or some

13

piece of productivity science they are lacking. You may feel this way too. Nothing could be further from the truth! You are simply not yet trained in managing and expressing yourself in a way that accomplishes what you desire *and* the experience of life that you want to have.

> *You are simply not yet trained in managing and expressing yourself in a way that accomplishes what you desire.*

Similarly, I have found it an odd notion to think about managing stress. We relate to stress like it is something that you catch, like a cold or the flu. A more appropriate moniker would be to learn to manage our "stress response." It is our response to outer circumstances that produces stress, more than the outer circumstances themselves (with a few exceptions such as big bears chasing you through the woods, bad guys breaking into your home, or other outer events that are wildly unusual and beyond our control). For the most part, what we are stressed about are the daily concerns of managing work, health, home and family. Our current stressors are not even close to being on the level of survival, but we unconsciously respond as if our very survival is at stake.

I have worked in the realms of psychotherapy, addictions and recovery, professional coaching, spirituality and personal transformation for nearly thirty years. I've worked with real people, and their lives, hurts, dreams and often troubling realities. I have seen what works and what doesn't. I've watched countless people try desperately to take up the practices of time and stress management to streamline their days, get more done, be more peaceful or successful, or all of the above. One after another, I've watched the techniques fail. It occurred to me years ago that the reason that stress and time management techniques don't work is because they deal with things that exist only as *external* concepts, outside of our control. Time and stress, and indeed all of the things that we try to manage, are mere dust clouds that we try to get our hands on and heads around.

I want to offer you a radically different view from what our culture tells you is true. I want to show you a paradigm shift away from managing time and stress toward managing your personal energy. In doing so, you will find and create new energy by which to live. However, only by taking a methodical approach will you be able to implement this in your life.

What does it mean to manage your energy rather than your time? Traditional methods of managing time focus on externals, as if time is something outside of you. The truth is that we live *in time* and how we move through and relate to time determines the quality of our experience in life. Author Max Strom teaches that we should live as if our time and our life spans are the same thing—because of course they are. How we spend our days is how we spend our lives. Yet how often do we find ourselves living a "someday" life? Someday I am going to slow down. Someday things will feel less chaotic. Someday I will be peaceful. Unfortunately, it is too often the case that "someday" never comes.

15

Moving through time includes two domains: your outer actions and activities; and your inner quality of being. For example, you can be on vacation and feel stressed and harried. (Have you ever gone to Disney World? Then you know what I am talking about!) Or you can be at work in complete peace and contentment. Outer activity does not unilaterally determine inner experience: it is the other way around. Once you begin to understand this truth, and add some incredible skills with managing the outer activity, you will begin living a new life, one of self-mastery and joy.

But I'm getting ahead of myself. For now, it is enough to say that managing energy versus time is a matter of managing inner states (what I call consciousness) and outer activity with excellence, clarity and intention.

Chapter Two

Setting Your Intention for Change

There is only one corner of the universe you can
be certain of improving, and that's
your own self.

~Aldous Huxley, author

You are reading this book for a reason. You are spending your time, energy, thought and attention because you want something to shift in your life. Here is the pitfall that most people make when starting any change process: they think that if they learn some new tool or technique, their lives will somehow get better. But here is the truth: *Knowledge does not produce change!* Before you get too discouraged about that statement, let me add this: Knowledge *applied* produces change. To truly get the most benefit from what I am sharing, to truly start calming the chaos of your life, I highly recommend you get a buddy or small group to go through this process with you. You will greatly benefit from having others to talk over this information with and to support you

> *Knowledge does not produce change. Knowledge applied produces change!*

in creating the new skills you will learn. It is also very powerful to have a place where you can be accountable for doing the work. This material is fun, challenging and stimulating, so having a small group of people doing this together only multiplies the adventure!

> *When you apply these principles, you will become the least stressed, most productive person you know!*

Once you apply the principles deeply into your life, you will become the least stressed, most productive person you can possibly be. You will develop a more empowered relationship with time. How can I say that? Well, I am in fact the least stressed, most productive person I know, and I have also taught thousands of people this approach over the past ten years, and have seen the same result time and time again. When you develop these skills and alter your inner being or consciousness, you will truly come to see there is more to life than getting things done. At the same time, you will recognize that you are able to get much more done! It is a big world out there! There is so much goodness to experience and explore. Yet there is also so much need. I believe that you are called to give more to life, to give your full self to all that life has to offer.

In my previous book, *What If it's Time for a Change?*, I wrote about how to sustain motivation for change by creating a "compelling why" that pushes you beyond your current experience and stretches you to grow even when the change process is no longer fun, new and sexy. The type of change we are now addressing is that kind of change. It will take effort, focus and commitment, but the benefits are truly life-changing.

A great place to begin is for you to determine and declare exactly what you want to get from reading this book and integrating its concepts. One of the later principles in this book is about knowing what your intentions are for your life. You can begin training yourself about living with intention now. Declare what you intend to experience and create by reading this book and doing the work involved in calming the chaos.

Write your intention here:

What I intend to create as a result of doing the work of calming the chaos in my life is (In other words, what do you want to get from reading this book!):

I want to bring aliveness, excitement meaningful life. Productive work that feels good. Utilizing my gift Bring clarity and organized life Style, simple and beautiful ad loving relationship. Happy

People experiencing their worthiness

Chapter Three

There is More to Life than Getting Things Done!

Our relationship to time is what it is because we lie to ourselves about what we are and what we can do, and we hide from ourselves what we are meant to be and what we are meant to serve.

~Jacob Needleman,
American philosopher and author of *Time and the Soul*

Calming the Chaos addresses the problems created when we lose our "centeredness" in order to look for happiness and fulfillment someplace other than within. People often misunderstand this to mean that outer circumstances have no bearing on our overall happiness and wellbeing, which, of course, for most people is not the case. It is interesting to note that at the very highest ways of being, what I call the highest levels of consciousness, this statement can be entirely true; one's outer circumstances have truly no bearing on one's happiness and wellbeing. Look at the spiritual masters of the world who were able to meet even death with peace, knowing that their lives were for a larger purpose. In that knowing, they met their fates with peaceful composure.

For the rest of us mere mortals, however, we need balance between a deep, rich and sustaining inner world that is met by (and in fact creates) a fulfilling, meaningful and

> *We are here to grow in consciousness to the highest possible levels of living and being.*

satisfying outer world. I would even go so far as to say that this ability to find stability, calm, meaning, purpose and peace in the face of any outer circumstance—to "hold our ontological ground" if you will—is perhaps the purpose of all humanity. We are to learn and grow in consciousness to the highest possible levels of living and being. That is a *huge* statement, so take a moment to digest that a bit.

The purpose of your life, and in fact of all of humanity, is simply and profoundly to grow in consciousness so that we are not tossed about like a bottle on a wave, having no solid ground, but we rise above the storms of life to truly know and live from the most elemental center of our being. And yes, to *be* all of this while still *doing* all that we do in life—the marriage, the kids, the careers, the friends, the hobbies.

In essence, is this a book about having it all? Perhaps. When you understand that "having it all" begins with an inner being that is unflappable. Having it all means realizing that you are here to explore, create and declare your own unique, individual path in life—no matter how conventional or off-the-beaten-path that looks. You are here to fully, freely and joyfully experience and express the fullness of You!

Given the pace of modern culture, you likely feel the need to re-center, to "get a grip" on the way your life is going. How often does it happen that you get to the end of a day or week and look back and wonder, "Where was I? What did I do?" You may be accomplishing success on every level—career, the car, the home and family—and yet feel that something is missing. In some way, you don't inhabit your days. You feel empty or dry or disconnected from what you do, what you have and, more importantly, who you are. Or you might struggle to keep up, hardly fitting in the requirements of life, no matter everything you *want* on top of that. Either way, the problem is the same. Somewhere along the way what you *do* has been separated from who you *are*. The result is that you have located your identity, your "who you are" in what you do. This is a solution that places *doing* before *being* and as such never actually connects you to the elemental nature of your being. And *that*–the truth and power of our Being–is what we all crave.

This is a fundamental distinction, and is the starting point of managing your personal energy rather than your time. It is a shift from a full-out, pedal-to-the-metal drive based on what you are doing to an inner focus of who you truly are, the "you" that wants to come forth. It is what I call "shifting your focus" from the *content* to the *context* of your life.

For the most part, we are a culture of people driven by our life content; that is, what we do, whom we know and what we own. There is nothing wrong with having great life content. In fact, it is awesome to bring components into your life that enhance your overall life experience! But when the content consumes the sole focus and purpose of your existence, sooner or later the content loses its meaning, its importance. Your life ends up feeling bankrupt, not in the financial sense (although that happens far too often as well), but in the existential sense—the sense of our meaning, fulfillment and being.

The shift, then, from content to context is crucial. As I mentioned earlier, by context I am referring to the inner elements of your life, such as your values, emotions, beliefs, attitudes, commitments and ways of being. The sum of all of these inner elements is what I call your "level of consciousness." *Your level of consciousness is how you see the world. It gives you your experience of the world,* but most often you have no clue how you see the world! When you only see the outer world, you are truly powerless to calm the chaos, because the chaos lives first within you, and then around you.

> *Your level of consciousness is how you see the world that gives you your experience of the world.*

We are so wrapped up in all of our doing and rushing to get things done and stay abreast of the constant information around us that we've lost what it means to really be human in the framework of our daily lives. We all have a purpose, a reason we're here on this earth, and that purpose is to know ourselves deeply and, most of all, to grow. Losing sight of this purpose results in gradually draining the energy out of your soul. You become disconnected from the important questions about who you are and what you love and what your heart longs to express.

When you leave these questions unasked and unanswered, time slips by and you lose what it means to be "present" in the living of your life.

Jacob Needleman, in his book *Time and the Soul*, writes that we have "forgotten how to bring to our day-to-day lives the essential question of who and what a human being is and is meant to be." We feel overwhelmed and lost in life because we have "lost touch with the mystery of time; that is to say, the mystery of our humanness, our being, our life and death." He continues, "... the pathology of our relationship to time can be healed only as we allow ourselves to be penetrated by the mystery of what we are beneath the surface of ourselves–by striving, that is, to remember our Selves" (2003). By this capital S "Self," Needleman is pointing to what I have described above; there is a part of each of us that exists beyond the rat race existence we are now living, that longs for depth of meaning, connection and expression, that is in fact our very Soul.

Living our lives without our Selves is a dangerous proposition. We can make money, raise a family and even rise to great heights of success, without being much more than what the Tibetan Buddhists call "Hungry Ghosts" ever eating, yet never satiated. Always craving "more time" but the "more" is never enough because we are never truly *there,* never really *present in the living of life.* We become merely an empty shell of a body moving through the world. We can create a life that looks happy from the outside, but it is entirely possible to live for a hundred years without accessing any of what it means to be truly *human*–to be the inner essence of our being, the complexity and soulfulness of our deepest identity.

Contemporary culture demands that we keep pace in a way that excludes any time, space or encouragement for our Selves to speak. And when we don't listen to the Self, we fail to actually *be and experience the life we have*. We act, we achieve, and we engage in constant, often mindless doing. But we don't inhabit our hours and our days. We leave our spirits on the outside of all that doing. As Needleman writes, "In the world as in oneself, time is vanishing because we have lost the practice of consciously inhabiting our life."

The problem with contemporary culture is that it is very shallow, and human life is not. To address this quandary, it is necessary to start thinking in a new way and then doing things differently; actually, looking at having different *behaviors as well as new and different thoughts*. As they say in the 12-Step programs such as Alcoholics Anonymous, if you keep doing what you've been doing, you're going to keep getting what you have been getting. There is more to life than getting things done—and it is great to get things done—particularly when you are engaged in doing things that are meaningful, that you have consciously chosen to spend your life energy on and that you value.

Let's talk about how to have this material be most effective for you, and how you will get the most out of it. *We're going to be talking about you beginning to take on new behaviors and beginning to actually live and think in a different way.* The best way for you to accomplish this is to work on this material a little bit at a time, digest the content, put the new practices in place, and integrate them into your thinking and how you manage your days. The most powerful way to do this is to take out your schedule right now and schedule four or five sessions over the next four to five weeks to work with this material. Remember, knowledge does not create change. *Knowledge applied creates change.* If you get into this material slowly over time, it will begin to work in you to create true transformation.

We live in a "quick fix" culture, but recognize that lasting behavior change takes time, practice and deep integration into your being. You have your current mental model as a result of years of conditioned programming and practice (i.e. seeing things the same way over time, reinforced by cultural beliefs and messages, leading to certain behaviors and emotions). That is going to take some "unlearning" and undoing. With persistence you will develop the skills and mental models to calm the chaos. This book is not a program to follow as much as it is a lifestyle to be developed. This is a new beginning, a turning point in the way you see, interact with and experience your life.

Section Two: Deepening Your Awareness as the Path to Change

Awareness is like the sun. When it shines on things,
they are transformed.

~Thich Nhat Han, Zen Buddhist Monk,
author, poet, peace activist

Chapter Four

Managing Energy is a Matter of Life or Death!

Here's a simple formula: No faith equals no miracles.

~Bruce Schneider,
Founder of Institute for Professional Excellence in Coaching and
author of *Energy Leadership*

Years ago, before I had a child or a spouse or a deep connection to my inner life—when my existence was still defined by my career, my competitive nature, and my gradually expanding investment portfolio—a chronic pain developed in my arm and elbow. On top of my hectic professional life, I played racquetball in a competitive league near my Central Massachusetts home. I'd always been an athlete, and racquetball had taken the role that basketball, soccer and softball used to play.

The ache in my elbow had started to extend down toward my fingers, then creep upwards over my bicep toward my shoulder. I knew it was tendonitis, but I ignored it for far too long. Weeks passed, and I kept competing. Before I knew it, I could hardly lift my arm. I couldn't use my right hand to move the mouse on my computer, brush my teeth, write or shift gears in my car. What started as a dull ache turned into constant pain, keeping me awake at night. My doctor couldn't do anything but send me to an orthopedic surgeon, who, not surprisingly, suggested surgery. But going under the knife didn't seem like an option I wanted to jump at, so when a friend suggested I try her acupuncturist, I decided it couldn't hurt (pardon the pun!).

I walked into the practitioner's office and found a short man with kind, brown eyes sitting behind a simple desk, filling out paperwork. It was decorated sparsely in deep reds and grays, with plants and books and framed photographs on the shelves. The acupuncturist greeted me with a warm handshake and welcomed me into the treatment room.

Throughout the treatment I laid perfectly still on his table, listening to the deep silence around me, broken only by the gentle noises of his movements about the room, and the soft sounds of his breathing blended with my own. I felt my body very clearly, head to toe, as if I'd sunk back into it after a long time of being absent, like awakening from a groggy sleep full of confusion and bad dreams. A headache I didn't even realize I'd had eased out of my forehead and jaw, and the muscles of my back and thighs relaxed. A minute could have passed, or an hour or a day; it was all the same. When he finished the treatment, the kind man told me I could sit up, handed me a glass of water, and told me to take my time and meet him in his office when I was ready.

As I sat there, sipping at the water and feeling the perfect stillness of the room ring out around me, I thought about how different I felt. Was it the acupuncture that made me so light and expansive, or was it simply the time to lie still in complete silence? I rarely did that without feeling like I should be doing something else. I swore I could feel my blood running through my veins. I opened and flexed my right hand; it ached, but I could move it for the first time in weeks.

Back out in the office with the practitioner, I sank into a soft blue chair and waited. He asked me how I felt, and I gestured uselessly in the air between us. He chuckled and nodded.

"Yes," he said, "that happens."

"What is it?" I asked. My mouth formed the words slowly, deliberately. "What makes me feel so… " I trailed off.

"People like you," he said, his voice soft and gentle, "often experience a sort of awakening in my room."

I paused and thought about that. "People like me?"

"Correct me if I'm wrong," he said, holding out his hands in supplication, "but I'd say you're the competitive type. Hard-working, focused, career-driven. No?"

"Type A," I said with a chagrined smile.

He laughed. I smiled and nodded my assent.

"Your energy," he said, "is heavier than most people who come in here, even the Type A's. I felt it as soon as you walked in. It hangs about you like a dark cloud. You felt … drained, weighty." I cocked my eyebrows, intrigued, slightly embarrassed.

"Say more?"

He sat up straighter and folded his hands on his desk, pausing for a moment, then continued. "You're living your life in a certain way," he said. "You're basing it all on doing, activity, being busy. You have no grounding, spiritual practice. You push forward always, focused on gain, getting ahead and proving yourself. Am I right about this?"

I thought for a moment, then nodded silently.

"All of that is draining your life force energy," he said. His words came out like he was telling me I needed to pick up milk on the way home. I must have looked confused because he went on. "You are not a body; you *have* a body. You're a being of energy. We all are. And the way you're living right now is draining that energy. It's diminishing you. You're letting it all seep away in your outer search for fulfillment. And you're in danger of losing it all."

"What does that mean?" I asked.

The man shrugged. His eyes looked sad as they studied my face for a moment. "You won't live long this way," he said finally. "You'll die young if you keep this up. Your elbow isn't the problem, it's a symptom." He gestured toward my arm. "Eventually, all of you will go in that direction."

I remember this moment so clearly because it marked a massive turning point in my life. He spoke those words so casually, so honestly, and they rang deep inside me to fill my whole being. When I went home that night, everything had changed. Being told you're going to die young has a way of snapping you to attention. It was as if someone had taken off my usual glasses and put on a different pair, through which I could see my life for what it really was. What once fed me suddenly felt like air; what I spent my time focusing on–the professional success, accomplishment and the material wealth–felt dry and empty and dull. That was the moment I became aware.

All true inner work and change must begin with awareness. It's necessary to open your eyes and look around at what your life *actually* looks like, not what you think it looks like, how you wish it looked or how you want it to look "someday."

Before that acupuncture session, I thought my life was full and successful and thriving. But afterwards, with my sight changed, I realized that it was actually anything but. I had plenty of clients in my therapy and coaching practice, plenty of successful investments and consulting contracts. I had a nice life, but who was I in all of that? What kind of being-ness did I hold? What did I care about? Was I happy? Was I living as my whole, truest, highest Self? As I asked myself all of these questions, the answers were telling. The difference between how I felt during and immediately after that session—when my energy was thrumming and clear and high—and how I felt on a normal daily basis, was a stark contrast; my usual days, in comparison, were pressured and disconnected. I started to understand the cloud that my acupuncturist described seeing on me as I entered his office. It hung on my shoulders and dragged me down. That wasn't happiness, joy, peace and fulfillment; it was a driven, frantic feeling that left me feeling only fractionally myself.

My point in sharing my story is this: we all must start with awareness. We have to take off the blindfold in order to proceed. This section will lead you toward a new way of seeing your life, which is the groundwork for learning to manage your energy rather than your time.

Chapter Five

Awareness of What You Say about Time

*The important thing to remember is that, in general,
our behavior does not reflect what
we really believe...*

~Hyrum Smith, Creator of the Franklin Day Planner and
author of *The 10 Natural Laws of Successful
Time and Life Management*

The concept of awareness is a huge topic in itself, but let's begin by looking at it from two very concrete perspectives: what you say about time (which reflects how you feel about time) and how you spend your time. One of the ways that we begin distinguishing our relationship with time is in the language we use to describe it. I have taught hundreds of seminars around this topic of calming the chaos and have asked this question to thousands of people, "What do you most often say about time?" What do you think I hear over and over again? What is your own answer? If you are like the scores of people in my seminar programs, the almost immediate answer is, "I don't have enough." We live with such a feeling of scarcity with regards to time. Here are a few of the other things I hear:

- I don't have time to do this or that.
- How am I going to find the time?
- Where did the time go?
- I'll make time later.
- This will save me some time.
- If only I had more time.

Can you imagine having a relationship with time where it is no longer doing something to you, but it is simply a resource that you have, and inside this resource you are living your life? Isn't that a very different paradigm? Time simply is, and you simply are. The more you relate to time as a resource or, in fact, time as an *opportunity*, the more you will feel empowered to make conscious choices with what to do with this resource. Time is not doing something to you. It is your *gift*.

Time is not disappearing, shrinking, running out or any other disempowering notion that you may have. Time merely exists for you, and your freedom begins when you interact with it in a new and different way.

Time is the medium of life! Life exists inside of your experience of time and, without it, you would not be living any longer. Read the accounts of people who have had near death experiences (NDE's) and you will read again and again that the whole construct of time completely changed for them as they "passed over" and then returned. On the "non-physical plane" there is no sense of linear time. It is a construct of our human experience on the physical plane. Therefore it is truly our gift. To engage with time in an empowered way is our reciprocation of this gift. Recognize the beauty and honor of living life awake to the mystery and uncertainty of time, and your relationship to time will be forever changed.

You will see how advertisers cash in on our contemporary time famine. "12 Time Saving Products for Busy Parents" is a featured article in BabyZone.com or the "10 Best Time Saving Appliances" is on *Forbes* magazine. Everywhere you look, you will find advertisers telling you that their latest and greatest products will save you time. What is the message here? No one has time to do what they need to do and you had better get on board with the latest and greatest device that will *save you time!* But time cannot be "saved" for use at some later date. Time just is!

Then there are the less formal, yet equally powerful messages that come from our daily interactions with friends and colleagues. What is the standard answer when you bump into a friend at the grocery store or the gym and ask "How you doing?" The seemingly automatic, robotic reply is, "Oh, I'm so busy!" This quip is generally followed by a five-minute soliloquy on the details of this busyness with something along these lines: "Oh, we've been so busy. Suzy is doing soccer, marching band and dance, and Joe is in football and swimming. We are on the family council at church, and the time it takes to get them each to their activities, get homework done and cook dinner leaves me wasted at the end of the day. I barely have time to clean up from dinner, make lunches and crawl into bed."

While "the disease du jour" of overwhelm is clearly more intense for working parents, don't think those who are single and child-less get off any easier. The litany of activities may look different, but the tenor of the message remains the same: "I've got a lot going on, and (read between the lines), therefore, I matter."

You have got to look to see where and to what degree you are playing the "I'm so busy" game as well. Do you find a sense of importance and self-esteem in how much you have going on, how many activities you do, how much your kids are doing? Where does it end? Yes, it is a big world out there; but remember, when you are a "yes" to everything, you will be a "no" to your peace of mind!

Chapter Six

Awareness of Our Cultural Paradigm about Time

It's not enough to be busy. Even the ants are busy.
The question is what are you busy about?

~Henry David Thoreau

As we can clearly see above, we are living in a cultural paradigm that values being busy and holds it in an oddly high esteem. There is a certain status and sense of importance of being busy, often, if not always, at the expense of living a life of meaning and fulfillment. Being booked up, busy and running full throttle all the time has become the cultural icon of a successful life. "Busy" as the new status symbol is wreaking havoc

> *Having it all has been up-leveled by doing it all!*

with the quality of our lives. It is what University of North Dakota researcher Ann Burnett calls the "busier than thou" attitude. "Keeping up with the neighbors'" now means having to out-schedule them. Having it all has been up-leveled by doing it all!

The primary cause of stress is being busily engaged in too many activities that have very little meaning to you! The busier you are, the more important you may feel; but the busyness is draining the life out of you. While you may now be recognizing that, chances are you don't know what to do about it. The resolution to this stress is to create meaning in what you are doing—or do something else! It also resides in developing your ability to simply *do less!*

We are so distracted with activity and technology and constant stimulation. We complain to others and ourselves that we need to slow down, to unplug and yet we do nothing about it. What is really behind all this busyness in our culture and in our minds? It is easy to think that the constant stream of media, information and activity causes the problem, but these are just external elements. They don't attack us like Alfred Hitchcock's *"The Birds."* The objects and activities of our world are just that—objects and activities. Objects that can be turned off (gasp!) or at the very least silenced for a time. Activities can be refused. The problem is not so much all that is coming at us, but in our growing inability to consciously choose what and when to engage with technology, media and the various other forms of non-stop stimulation. We say we are a distracted nation, but aren't we all blaming external conditions for our inner turmoil?

Technology is not going to disappear or slow down. The opportunities for learning, service, fitness, travel, employment and entertainment will likely not dry up anytime soon. Short of moving to some remote island, *learning how to manage the input and stimuli seems the only sure path forward.* Managing the input has more to do with beginning to understand what truly feeds you, what truly has meaning and what you can begin, ever so slowly, to remove from your life because it simply does not elevate and energize you.

Lack of meaning is a cultural epidemic. Negotiating the tension between cultural expectations and the cry of your heart requires tenacious resiliency. Dr. Brene Brown states in her research on vulnerability that we are the most overweight, overmedicated and addicted generation in history. I firmly believe that there is a direct correlation between our cultural obsession with busyness devoid of meaning, and this rising epidemic. We are so busy that we no longer think or feel or connect. This lack of meaning and belonging leaves us starved for something that we largely no longer use our time for–connection with community, connection with nature, connection with the spiritual world, connection with our own inner voice. To mask the desperation, we eat, we drink, we numb out on endless media and all manner of activity that further our sense of inner and outer alienation.

My TEDx talk was directed exactly at this cultural conundrum. In this talk, titled, "Creating Conscious Communities," I point to the lack of communal identity in our current culture and address a few strategies to address that. When we feel starved for time, we draw back from connections to those around us, which only serves to drive us further away from the feeling of value and meaning. One of the key strategies I address in the talk rests in moving from frantically overwhelmed to fully present. The path to conscious connected communities lies in our ability to calm the chaos. You can view the entire TEDx talk at https://www.youtube.com/watch?v=Wgzx9rkNxso.

Chapter Seven

Awareness of How You Use Your Time

The proper function of man is to live, not to exist. I shall not waste my days in trying to prolong them. I shall use my time.

~Jack London, author

I worked with a coaching client back in 2012 who hired me due to his increasing distress over his relationship with his supervisor. He reported having difficulty getting along with her, and that she was always "on his back about being late to work." That seemed like a simple enough issue to me, and it perplexed me as to why he would want to hire a coach to work on this, as it seemed very straightforward and simple. But this was clearly a man who was committed to his career and wanted to do well in life, so I accepted his invitation to work with him as his professional coach.

The first place I went to work was where all change begins: dealing with his awareness of his behavior. This occurred through the simple question; "She says you are chronically late to work. What time do you get there?"

"Usually around 8:45-9:00," came his deadpan reply.

"And what time does your work day start? Is there an understanding that you have to maintain certain hours?"

The reply came, albeit not in a straightforward fashion; he did work in a culture that was fairly clear that the workday runs from 8:30-5:00. I pointed out to him that in fact his boss was correct. He was, upon his own admission, routinely late for work. He agreed that perhaps the issue was not his boss, but the fact that despite numerous attempts, he simply could not get himself to work before 8:30.

This was probably the simplest coaching structural intervention in the history of the coaching profession, but within the week, my client had solved the issue. What was the intervention? I simply had him do a time study and keep track of what he was doing and when he was doing it. The outcome? He learned that he had, for many years, allotted himself 30 minutes to get up, shower, make coffee and get out of the house to get to work when in fact it took him about 45-55 minutes to do his morning routine. He was simply unaware of this discrepancy. He *believed so strongly* that it took him 30 minutes, that he could not even see that it was taking him nearly an hour.

This may sound ridiculous and simplistic to you, but I promise that you have similar areas in your life that you are equally unconscious about time. We truly have very little clue as to how long things actually take us, and hence we are chronically late or stressed out to get to places on time or meet our deadlines (yes, I am living proof of this as I finish this book right up against my deadline to my editor!). Awareness of how we actually use time, how long things actually take is one of the first pieces of awareness you need to develop in order to calm the chaos.

So for the next seven days, track your time in 15-30 minute increments so that you wake up to the realization of how you spend your time and how long things actually take. There is power in awakening to the truth of how you use this resource that we call time.

Try not to change anything as you do this tracking exercise! Don't all of a sudden stop watching TV or losing mindless minutes on social media, don't get up earlier to do the exercise you have been meaning to do; simply live your life the way you have been living it, but track how you *actually* spend your time versus how you think you do or wish you would. Track your activities as closely as possible. For example, if you are at work for eight hours, do not simply write the time of those eight hours and jot down "work." This will not give you the specifics to actually become aware of how you are spending your time. Write down something closer to this:

- 8:00—Arrive at work, get coffee, check email
- 8:30—Meet with Jane about next week's program
- 10:00—Talk to Steve about the company picnic
- 10:15—Respond to emails, call pet sitter about next weekend, start on report
- 10:45—Deal with client emergency
- 12:00—No idea what I did in the past hour! (Yes, that will happen, I promise you!)
- ... and so on throughout your day and into the evening until bed.

47

This log is for YOU. It is to gain awareness of where you are effective with regard to managing yourself in time and where you are not. Fill out your log *at least* five times during the day, but preferably every 15-30 minutes. If you wait to do it at the end of the night, you will not have any clear sense of how you actually spent the day.

There are numerous methods you can use for the actual data tracking. You can use an Excel spreadsheet, a small paper tablet that you keep with you, your Memo Pad function on your smartphone or apps that you can download that are time tracker apps. Whatever method you choose, just choose one and stick with it. Keep all your data in one place so you can have a solid log of information at the end of the week.

Keep in mind that I have no judgment about how you spend your time (although you very likely do!). You are certainly a competent, accomplished, successful person or you wouldn't be reading this book. You are up to something in life. You want more from life and you long to bring *more to* life. What I bring is a desire and commitment to help you use your energy in a way that feels better and results in you experiencing life in a higher, more powerful way — that you like yourself better and that you are happier with who you are at the end of the day. That is my commitment to you.

The goal and gift of doing a time log is that it is merely data. Try not to change your behavior because you are monitoring yourself (although just doing monitoring often helps people be more productive!). At the end of the week look to see where you are draining off time and effectiveness unconsciously.

You will learn a great deal about yourself, and in this chapter, as in all life change, there is power to awareness and clarity!

Chapter Eight

Awareness of How You
Use Your Energy

*You can turn over a new leaf every hour
if you choose.*

~Arnold Bennett, English novelist

A good place to begin our journey is to define what I mean when I use the term energy. In cultures and religions around the world, particularly in the East, there is a commonly held belief that part of our essence is purely energetic. Judith Orloff writes in her book, *Positive Energy*, that the Western and Eastern worlds conceive of energetic states, exchanges and experiences in varying ways:

While Westerners may consider subtle energy esoteric or New Age, it's been central to many healing traditions for millennia. I liken our society's response to the proverbial elephant in the living room; it's right in front of us, but we can't see it. In Chinese medicine, subtle energy is called *chi* or *qi*. It's *mana* to Hawaiian kahunas, *prana* to Indian Yogic practitioners and in Ayurveda, *ni* to Native

> *You can begin making choices that support your energy rather than drain your energy.*

Americans, *num* to African shamans, biofields to American scientists, and morphic fields to a growing renegade breed of international physicists and biologists. For me, there's something deeply amiss in a culture that utterly lacks a power word for the multifaceted energy so many belief systems presume we are.

Western culture is just starting to tap into a vast wealth of knowledge that's been intuited, studied and practiced in other parts of the world for thousands of years. Dr. Candace B. Pert explains that ancient cultures around the world "have always held that consciousness came first, followed by manifestation in the physical universe." It's nothing new, in Eastern thought, that "consciousness precedes the material world, and in fact is at the source of what we can see and touch." In our Western philosophies, however, including but not limited to medicine, it's believed that the physical world comes first, and our consciousness—our thoughts, ideas and emotions—develops out of that. What we are starting to learn is that it is the other way around. It turns out that our consciousness, our energy has immensely more power over our physical reality than we ever knew.

The best way that Western thought embraces the concept of energy is through science, namely in physics and biology. As we "feel" our many emotions (happiness, sadness, anger, desire, satisfaction....), the cells of our body literally begin to vibrate at frequencies corresponding to those emotions. Their vibration attracts certain chemicals that then connect with the cells' receptors and trigger physiological reactions. In her book *Everything You Need to Feel Go(o)d*, Pert calls this system the "bodymind," which challenges the division that Western science has placed between our psychology and our physiology. Our emotions and thoughts literally set our cells to buzzing, which in turn sets off complex strings of "psychosomatic" (literally, of-mind-and-body) manifestations through our bodies, created by those vibrations and subsequent chemical reactions.

The result is physical experiences of emotions, be it making oneself sick with guilt or the heart-pumping thrill of falling in love. In much more subtle ways, we are walking embodiments of the emotions that take place within us, vibrating and chemicalizing a thousand different thoughts and feelings and hopes a day. Consciousness, it seems, comes *first*, as it molds the body's experience. Our thoughts, emotions, beliefs and attitudes (our context) are waves of energy that create physical realities. Unfortunately, far too often, our context remains unconscious or "undeclared" in any tangible way and we thus end up "inheriting" the default context of our culture. And the current default is overwhelm and chaos.

Energy exchanges are experienced in very concrete ways. Imagine that the person at the desk beside yours in the office is feeling her recent divorce through intense waves of sadness, anger and guilt. Neurobiology and psychopharmacology tell us that her cells will be literally vibrating in frequency with those emotions. Your own cells are capable of picking up those "vibratory actions" through something called "cellular resonance." Her energy carries across space to affect your cells "like when you pluck one string on two different guitars in the same room—one will resonate with the other, both striking the same note," as Pert explains.

Quantum mechanics says that our particles, which make up our cells, are also vibrating constantly, at frequencies that express our energetic states and communicate to other particles in the world around us. According to these two sciences, you will likely feel your co-worker's angst and pain, even if you aren't interacting with her. You can feel the energy she gives off, or her "vibes," if you will.

All of this is a heavy load for the modern mind to wrap itself around, as it contradicts much of the scientific paradigm in which we were raised. But even we laypeople in the West have ways of understanding this exchange of energy; we intuit much more than we know how to scientifically explain. Remember, for instance, meeting someone for whom you had an instant affinity. You were drawn to them from the start, whether a romantic partner or friend—but what was it that pulled you to them? We often use terms such as "she had good energy," or "I got a good feeling from him," or "she has such a lightness, I love being around her." Conversely, you've probably experienced *bad* feelings around some people; they "rub you the wrong way." Maybe it's just "bad chemistry."

We sense energies in places, too. Call to mind the feeling you have in a bookstore versus a department store; a health food store versus a fast-food restaurant; a rural field full of sunlight versus a busy city street. We can walk into a space and get a feel from it without any previous knowledge of what it's all about. Many people talk about the "low morale" in the workplace, and when you go into such workplaces, the energy or the feeling of negativity is palpable. Without consciously recognizing it, we experience energies around us and internalize them into our very being. We are living in what I call "survival consciousness" where everyone feels that they are maxed out and running on all cylinders all the time.

When you are unconscious and do not create your own unique context of how you want to experience life, then you will unconsciously align with and live in the predominant consciousness that is around you. It is the nature of consciousness; without attending to how you want to feel and experience life, you will very likely have your experience of life molded for you by the predominant level of consciousness (i.e. "mass consciousness").

Herein lies the core of this book: when you become aware of energy and begin to consciously incorporate higher, lighter, more peaceful energies, and less of the low, stressful, chaotic energies, you literally experience life differently *and* create a different life.

It's that simple. But it's not that easy.

Section Three: Energetic Consciousness

We do not see things as they are. We see them as we are.

~Anais Nin, author

Chapter Nine

Understanding Consciousness and Its Role in Your Life

The only way you will allow new information into your consciousness is when your will to change is greater than your fear of change.

~Howard Falco, author of
I AM: The Power of Discovering Who You Really Are

Consciousness research is a growing field combining biology, psychology, ontology, neurology, philosophy, theology and even mysticism. Understanding energetic consciousness is truly the next frontier of the human potential movement. I am passionate about the promise of this new evolution of our human capacities. As the fields of science and spirituality continue to merge and learn from one another, the advances are crucially important for us to turn the tide away from the ever increasing levels of stress, overwhelm and anxiety and the increased sense of uncertainty. How can we turn this tide? How can we restore sanity to our non-stop, hurry-up, stimulation-driven world?

I believe the answer to these questions—as well as to more personal ones, such as, "How do I feel better in my day-to-day life?" or "How can I feel a greater sense of meaning, purpose and connection?"—lie in our pursuing this new domain where science and spirituality meet, the domain of energetic consciousness.

Let's start with the first word of that phrase. What is energy? Energy is the pattern of movement created by molecules in motion. It is that simple. Everything has energy–trees, cars, garbage, the ocean, people, thoughts (yes, thoughts too!), your pets, your furniture and every living and non-living thing on the planet. Literally everything vibrates with either higher/faster or lower/slower frequencies. I'm sure you have come across this notion in some science program over your lifetime. It is also very intuitive. Which has a higher/faster vibration, water or a stone? I'm sure you answered water. It is clear that water is easier to mold and impact rather than a stone. The same is true of your thought and emotional energy. The higher/faster your emotional energy, the easier it is to shift and change all kinds of things in your life. Let me ask you to rely on your intuitive sense again. Which emotion has the higher vibration–anger or love, compassion or condemnation? Again, I'm sure you were able to look at these comparisons and recognize that love and compassion "resonate" at a higher level than anger and condemnation. As you begin to understand the energy of your inner world, you have shifted into the domain of energetic consciousness.

> *Consciousness is the energetic field inside of which you live and move and have your being.*

Once you grasp the idea of energy, next it is powerful to realize that you *have* a level of consciousness. Too often people go through their entire lives without realizing that they interact with their world from inside a set of beliefs and perceptions about why things are as they are–and this set of beliefs and perceptions affects every single thing they do, from grocery shopping to career choices to falling in love. This way of seeing the world is what I call your level of consciousness. An even more profound truth is that you have the power to change your level of consciousness.

What is energetic consciousness? There are so many varying definitions of this concept, from the medical field to physics to philosophy. Academic neurosurgeon and author of *Proof of Heaven* Dr. Eben Alexander writes that consciousness is the most profound mystery in the universe. That will give you some indication of the profound and complex nature of this esoteric phenomenon.

One common definition is that consciousness means awareness–to be conscious means that you are aware. The question though is to be aware of what? While I agree that awareness is key, you must be able to simultaneously be aware of your outer and inner states. Managing energetic consciousness rests in managing your inner states as they exist and as you relate to the outer world.

My definition of consciousness is that it is the energetic resonance or vibratory field created by the total of your thoughts, emotions, beliefs, perceptions, attitudes and ways of being. It encompasses the mental, emotional and spiritual aspects of an individual. It is a state of awareness, yet one's level of consciousness surpasses merely being aware of emotions and thoughts. It is in fact the sum total of one's inner world. Consciousness is the energetic field inside of which you live and move and have your being. Change your consciousness and you literally change the way you see the world, which of course changes what you experience.

Understanding energetic consciousness is not necessarily mystical, nor is it dogmatic, or grounded in any religious orientation. Energy does not show favor to any philosophy, creed or science. Consciousness is engaged in a very real and practical way with human evolution; how we, as human beings, grow and evolve over the whole of time. As we evolve as a human species, I believe that our consciousness, our conscious capacities to understand and manage energy are increasing.

Let's take the esoteric theory and make it practical. Years ago, I worked with a non-profit mental health organization to set up a supported housing program for young men transitioning out of the foster care system. These men were incredibly abused and neglected as children, and most of them had bounced around from foster home to foster home for many years. You can only imagine the impact that the lack of stability, love and guidance had on these young men, not to mention the horrific abuse they suffered earlier in life that landed them in state care in the first place.

One afternoon, one of the young men—I'll call him Beck—came into the living room after our staff meeting to find out if his weekend pass had been approved. He had been showing signs of increased agitation over the week, and with his history of serious violence, including nearly killing someone with a baseball bat, we felt we needed to keep a close eye on him so his pass was denied. When Beck learned this news, he exploded in an angry rage and started across the room at me. The program director bolted past me into the office and quickly dialed 911. Beck continued past me, making a bee-line for the office, grabbed the phone from the program director, pulled it out of the wall and turned to come at me with the phone receiver held over his head, about to use it as a weapon. Mind you, Beck was six-foot-two and 195 pounds. I am five-foot-seven and fairly petite in stature. In other words, he could have broken me in two like a toothpick.

It was one of those moments when time stands still. I knew this was a life-changing moment for Beck: If he slammed my head in with the phone receiver, there would be a very good chance he would go to jail for most of his adult life. If he calmed himself down and regained control, there was a very good chance that he would stay in the program to continue the recovery work that he so desperately needed. In an instant I saw his future, while also being keenly aware of keeping the

> *How you respond in any moment is determined by your level of consciousness.*

staff and other residents safe, and also knowing that my safety was in grave danger. I knew without a doubt that how I responded would make a world of difference in this situation. And *how I responded in that moment was entirely determined by my consciousness—what I was thinking, feeling, saying and believing in that moment.* If I responded in a consciousness of fear, anger and defensiveness, it would result in one outcome and if I responded in a consciousness of peace, love and acceptance, it would produce a different outcome for this young man and myself.

I truly believe that when you operate in the highest realm of consciousness (we will go into what that means in a second), it becomes the realm of grace; the energetic realm where miracles happen, and what happened next with Beck is a demonstration of that. I looked him in his wild brown eyes, I saw the veins in his neck pulsing outwards, his hand tense around the telephone handle, and with the calmest, softest of voices, I said over and over, "Beck, it's OK. I'm not going to fight with you. You are OK. You can do better than this. Relax. It's going to be OK." I just kept repeating these statements while softening my body as I faced him; after a moment or two (which felt like an hour), his shoulders slumped, his muscles relaxed, he threw the phone to the floor and stormed past me. Just as he reached the front door, the police arrived. Beck did not fight them, he simply gave them his hands to be cuffed and was taken out of the program without incident.

How does this relate to energetic consciousness? I believe, and consciousness research has shown, that when a person brings a high enough energetic vibration to a situation, it can literally transmute lower consciousness energies. In other words, my staying in calm, loving, accepting energy near Beck helped him to come back to his own center, to make a better, higher choice, and in fact I believe changed the course of his life. He somehow felt the power of this very high energy, and knew that anger and violence were not going to lead him anywhere.

When Beck came back into the program, he was different somehow; he was less combative, less aggressive in his mannerisms and way of being. He went on to get a job, finish high school and eventually transition to living in the community independently, despite his incredibly troubling start at life. High-consciousness energy is indeed the domain of grace.

Chapter Ten

Like Attracts Like on the Energetic Plane

We are all building our lives from the intentions and contents of our consciousness.

~Rev. Roger Teel, Mile Hi Church, Colorado

My intention is to convey the *very first steps* in creating a practical understanding of energetic consciousness. You have power over your life and how you experience it, but in order to do so, you must develop a greater awareness for the energies around and within you. Here is an example of what occurs when like attracts like on the energetic plane:

I have a dear friend named Tony, who by all external appearances is a highly successful man. He is a self-made millionaire, hasn't needed to work since his mid-forties and owns several luxury properties in highly desirable locations. He has all of the toys and freedom that money can buy–yet he is one of the unhappiest friends I have and attracts some of the most difficult people and circumstances into his life I've ever seen. A recent example brought this home for me.

Tony owns and manages rental units and consequently needs to deal with contractors on a regular basis. We were on the phone one day, and he was lamenting about the poor service he receives from service technicians and contractors. I was doing some home renovations at the time and it was striking to me that I had literally not one glitch or service problem with the entire renovation (and I was serving as my own general contractor, something known to be a nightmare by most standards!). I even had a Home Depot salesman come to my home because I was having difficulty with the equipment I had rented from them. He came over, *on his own time,* to show me how to properly use the equipment and stayed well into the evening to help with my wood floor project! Like attracts like on the energetic plane!

As you elevate your consciousness, you can change your "vibratory resonance;" as you do so, you change what you attract into your life. You come closer to your innate perfection, or what I call your "God-Self on earth." You literally become more attractive (not physically, although I swear that happens too). But by attractive I mean you create the energetic conditions for that which you desire to be brought toward you (attracted to you). You can achieve more, experience more joy, love, success and peace. This is not simply because "if you believe it you can achieve it." It is much more complex than that, and anyone who has ever tried simply changing what you believe knows this to be true.

There is indeed tremendous power to changing your beliefs; but the bigger picture that is too often overlooked is that changing your beliefs helps to elevate your consciousness. As you elevate your consciousness, you literally begin creating the energetic conditions to bring forth the experiences you desire, rather than the ones that you spend so much time complaining about! What you think about you bring about, because what you think about directly corresponds to the vibratory pattern of your energetic consciousness.

These concepts are so exciting for me because I truly believe that understanding how to elevate energetic consciousness is our hope for humanity. I believe this is true because any time any one of us grows and expands in consciousness, all of humanity changes. This is

> *Any time any one of us grows in consciousness, all of humanity changes.*

because we are energetic beings living in an energetic universe. We are all connected to one another through an intricate web of energetic consciousness. As you grow, we grow—and that is the purpose that we are all here to achieve.

So, you might ask, *how* do you evolve in consciousness? Well, I suppose one could say that's the purpose of this book. Shifting your energy and changing your consciousness is not an easy task. Altering your predominant model of thought is a much vaster undertaking than just understanding that you have a consciousness, though awareness is a great start, and necessary to any further work. You have to look at both the macro and micro levels, at the way society operates and what it tells you is true, and also at the way you internalize that and use it to empower or disempower your life. Then you have to begin to change your way of thinking, perceiving, interacting and responding to life.

We are grounded in routine, because routines are comfortable, safe, familiar. But in order to actually change the way you experience life, you have to be willing to shake things up a bit. You have to take a good hard look at the unconscious ways you process the world, the things you tell yourself, your ongoing assumptions, the places you use your precious energy. You have to identify what's most important to you, what you value beyond all else, what sets a fire in your belly, and what you desire. And then you have to be willing to change, and that requires stepping into the unknown, the unfamiliar, where you aren't sure if the ground is sturdy or not.

Calming the chaos requires paying attention to how you are using and managing the energy within and around you. Remember the acupuncturist who told me that my life force energy was strikingly low for someone as young as I was at the time? I needed to learn how to pay attention to my energy —what was feeding me, what was draining me— and how to create an increased flow of positive energy into my life.

Same Circumstance, Different Experience

The same situations, challenges and opportunities can occur to two different people, but will only be experienced through the predominant level of consciousness of each person. Let me tell you a story to highlight this point. I had a coaching client years back who had the experience of inheriting around $250,000 when her father deceased. My client is wonderfully engaged, happy and vital. She is someone that you might call a high-energy person. She has a sister who is frequently negative and complaining, often having health challenges, carrying a more negative view of people and life in general. She is someone you might consider to be a lower-energy person. Both women inherited the same amount of money, yet upon learning of their inheritance they had radically different responses.

My client, Sabrina, was elated. She was grateful to her parents for planning and providing for her in this way and quickly went about deciding what to do with the funds. She made plans to pay off her daughter's last two years of college, put some money in her retirement account and happily planned a two-month tour of Europe. Her sister on the other hand, received this gift with marked consternation. She complained that her parents could have helped her more when they were younger, that she cannot trust anyone to invest the money for her and that "now everyone would want something" from her. Mind you, this woman lived in a run-down mobile home that was in disrepair and drove an old, broken-down car. She was not a woman without financial need, but she could only receive and experience this gift through her predominant level of consciousness.

Whenever you experience an elevation in consciousness you break away from limiting belief systems and attitudes. Growing in consciousness is similar to getting corrective lenses and being able to see the world more clearly. *Moving through life at an elevated level of consciousness is the key factor in leading a life of happiness, peacefulness, joy and success.* This is very simple in concept – and yet not at all easy in practice.

Your level of consciousness creates your world each moment. Your overall happiness, satisfaction and peace of mind expand as your awareness and knowledge of your level of consciousness grow. It is the lens through which you view your world. By elevating your consciousness, you can create a more powerful, fulfilling and rewarding life.

Chapter Eleven

Change Your Consciousness, Change Your Life

Consciousness is the highest word you will ever
utter. Nothing is higher or deeper
than consciousness.

~Michael A. Singer, author of
The Untethered Soul: A Journey Beyond Yourself

Let me share another example to keep making this notion of consciousness practical and easy for you to apply to your own life.

I was recently teaching these concepts at a seminary institute where a student, Alicia, was looking ahead to her next semester with marked trepidation regarding the demands of the workload. She was lamenting over her upcoming schedule since every week on Wednesdays, she would need to go from her internship straight to her classes, meaning she would have about a 12-hour, non-stop day, with her only breaks being her drive time to and from her home, internship location and school. She was adamant that it was going to be horrible, that she wouldn't even be able to eat, that she would grow light-headed, irritable and it might impact her ability to perform well and possibly even to graduate. She was angry that the evening course was added to her schedule and felt that the registrar was doing this to her. She was anxious and felt victimized by the upcoming semester.

Having learned the levels of consciousness the day before, Alicia was aware of the concept and yet, here she was in the thick of it. I asked her what level of consciousness her thinking represented. She reluctantly admitted that she was exhibiting lower consciousness.

"What else is possible?" I queried.

"I don't know. I mean it is going to be challenging, if not horrible. But that's just the way it is in seminary. It is challenging. We are being trained to deal with things like this," came her quick reply.

"Is that the truth? Like an observable phenomenon?" I persisted.
"Well, it is *my* truth," she asserted.

"Yes, I can see that. What experience is that creating for you?"

"It's stressful. It makes me feel angry and stressed."

"Yes, that is right. Let me ask you, what else is possible?"

"I don't know. It's just going to be hard," came her resigned reply.

"If you *did* know, what would the answer be?" (That is one of my favorite coaching questions that always leads to greater insight and possibility!).

"Well, I suppose I could pack a cooler before I leave in the morning and bring healthy food with me so I am not starved all day," she stated as she began to waiver in her adamant proclamation that it was going to be horrible and challenging.

"Yes, you could. But let me ask you, why do this at all? Why bother going through a 12-hour day with very little breaks and packing your cooler to bring your food along and maybe even having to eat in the car? Why do it?"

"Because I want to be ordained. I want to be a minister," came her heartfelt reply.

"Yes, you do. And in service of that higher commitment, how can you relate to and experience your days on Wednesdays rather than suffering through them?"

"I can recognize that I have chosen this, and therefore, I can choose to have Wednesdays be a better experience too," she said as her face lightened.

"Yes, you can, and I know you will."

She shifted how she perceived the Wednesday experience, and as she did so everything changed. She moved from feeling victimized by her schedule to feeling empowered by her

> *As you elevate your consciousness, your experience of life changes.*

choices and in fact by her overall life mission. I don't know too many things that are more empowering than that.

As this example demonstrates, as we shift and elevate through the levels of consciousness, our experience of life changes. What are the levels of consciousness and how does consciousness impact people? I have spent years studying this topic and have created a simple, four-level model based on the in-depth work and research of other consciousness experts. The late Dr. David Hawkins was a pioneer in the understanding and measuring of human consciousness. He developed a 17-level model that detailed various consciousness experiences in life. Similarly, Dr. Bruce Schneider created a 7-level model of consciousness that was validated by research he conducted measuring the ways in which various people perceive the world. I simplified these two models into a 4-level model to make it easy to understand and apply to daily life. Here is a description of these four levels.

Level 1: Survival

The name given to Level One Consciousness (L1C) is "Survival" because it reflects just that–a notion of just getting by and surviving life. It is very difficult to live in or be around. This energetic consciousness is marked by the notion that "life is hard." There is a strong tendency toward "victim" thinking with a tendency to blame others and external events for conditions and circumstances. L1C includes thoughts and feelings of despair, resignation, sadness, self-doubt and low self-esteem (in general, or in any particular aspect of life such as work or relationships). There is a sense of apathy regarding one's plight and passivity toward improving one's condition or circumstances because "it is just too hard" to get in action to improve the situation. A person who persistently lives in this level mostly feels powerless to impact life and therefore takes very little initiative attempting to make things better. There are often unhealthy lifestyle choices associated with this level such as "numbing" behavior because of the belief that life is so hard. Numbing behavior can include things such as an increased tendency to indulge in unhealthy eating, excessive use of media, alcohol, drugs and overspending. Emotionally, L1C feels draining and tiring, and the amount of desire, engagement, and action is very low. It is a highly unproductive and unpleasant state of consciousness.

From a L1C perspective, there is a strong tendency to look for help and assistance from others rather than engage in activities that might improve conditions; and yet, a near constant rejection of such help, particularly if the help comes in the form of suggestions for change. Such suggestions would likely be met with, "You just don't understand." Thus, at this level, people often avoid active engagement with life, personal growth or trying to better their circumstances. At this level of consciousness, people don't like the way their lives are, and yet are fairly resigned about it. They could aptly be called "negaholics" given their constant propensity toward negative thinking. The near constant negativity is draining to the people living this way and to others around them. Fatigue is a near constant companion, and makes higher-level accomplishments difficult.

The focus in L1C is "fully outer" focusing on what is wrong or what is hard "out there" with other people and circumstances. The classic iconic example of this is visiting a prison where no one is guilty! Everyone is there because the cop was out to get them or the judge was a jerk or the lawyer didn't do his job. At L1C, there is very little self-awareness and one's perceptions are focused on what is happening in the outer world.

Level 2: Stress

Level two consciousness (L2C) is named "Stress" which results in the continued experience that life is hard, but with the belief that if one works hard enough, long enough, maybe something can be done about it. This energy is also quite difficult to be around and to live in, as there is barely any room for ease, pleasure, relaxation and rest (because of the belief that one has to "work hard to get ahead"). L2C contains thinking of struggle, antagonism and competition. There is anger and frustration at "having to work so hard to get ahead." Many people live in this difficult energetic consciousness that leads to frequent stress, unhappiness, overwhelm and anxiety.

Those who resonate at this level use forceful approaches in interacting with others, such as intimidation, passive aggressive styles and coercion. They tend to be hard workers and can be quite driven. There is a tendency to be critical of self and others, and to do a lot of finger pointing and condemnation. Similarly, people who live in this energetic consciousness are prone to worry, and tend to be chronic "what if" thinkers.

The focus at L2C is primarily directed outward towards other people and events, but there may be times of self-reflection at the higher end of L2C. The predominant focus of energy and conversation is on what is happening "out there" but with some guidance and support, there can be a shift to begin reflecting on how the person with L2C may have contributed to the difficult circumstances.

Level 3: Transformation

Level three consciousness (L3C) is the first level where people begin to experience life beyond the notion that "life is hard" and thus is called "Transformation." It is at this that people begin to enjoy life, experience greater success and offer greater contribution to the world. People at this level have a strong desire for personal improvement, success and making a contribution (which may sometimes be their nemesis).

At this level, people enter into what Bruce Schneider calls "anabolic" rather than "catabolic" energy (*Energy Leadership: Transforming Your Workplace and Your Life from the Core, 2007*). By anabolic energy, Schneider is referring to energetic consciousness that is life sustaining rather than draining. Anabolic energy (levels three and four) is generative, clear and constructive whereas catabolic energy (levels one and two) tends to instill greater difficulty, hardship and chaos.

At the lower range of L3C people may still have some sense that life is hard, but they feel optimistic that they can and will make progress toward success in life. They have goals. They are willing to be responsible for the way their life looks rather than blame other people or circumstances for the outcomes they are producing.

At the higher range of L3C people are very self-empowered. They operate with clarity and direction nearly all the time, and are very consistently setting and achieving new goals and personal standards.

People with L3C make great leaders because they are not only willing to go the extra mile, but also because their positive energy is so infectious that others almost always come along. They are responsible, reliable and committed to creating positive outcomes for themselves and others.

People who resonate with L3C are skilled listeners because their energy is empathic and attuned to other people. They have less personal ego to defend and are therefore more open to the needs, input, feelings and feedback of others.

Level 4: Transcendence

Level four consciousness (L4C) is deeply inspirational, peaceful and creative. It is called "Transcendence" because people who live at this level of consciousness truly transcend life's everyday cares and concerns. They are able to impact large masses of people with very little action because they can *cause* events without all of the work and effort that must occur at the lower levels. The locus of their power rests in their energy, wisdom, clarity and intention. They are aligned with the flow of life, and the universal laws of manifestation.

People with L4C are often spiritual leaders or leaders of great movements such as Gandhi, Mother Teresa and Nelson Mandela. They move through life with awe and sacredness and are profoundly present to the experience of life. People who resonate at L4C are filled with unconditional love and experience a certain oneness or unity with humanity and all of life. They are curators of deep and harmonious relationships, even in the face of radical disagreement or conflict (stopping wars, ending violence and seeking justice). It is truly a rare individual who lives at this high energetic consciousness, but their impact and role in the world is beyond measure.

The focus of L4C is entirely on the inner expression in life. Outer circumstances and events are of little consequence to the person living in L4C. The people who live in this consciousness experience nearly constant inner peace. They live the notion that life is always unfolding in perfect order and harmony, therefore there is never any experience of strain, pressure or stress.

Their energy is so attractive and generative that they often have large followings of devotees (such as Christ or Buddha). The outcomes that get produced at this level leave the average human baffled. It is truly the realm of miracles.

Each of us has a level of consciousness that we embody at any given time that fluctuates slightly depending on a variety of factors such as surroundings, physical needs such as fatigue or illness, and external demands. Our level of consciousness is not static, but varies according to these and other factors. For example, I belong to a church with fantastic music, enthusiastic participants, a vibrant minister and a tight-knit community. Within the walls of our sanctuary the people sway and clap to the music, the big windows let in bright light and paintings in vibrant colors brighten the walls.

Vases overflow with flowers and the high ceilings offer expansiveness and air. When I'm in that space, in the midst of an uplifting service with lots of laughter and singing and centeredness among the congregants, I feel my energy soar. It is almost as if someone wraps a harness around me and pulls me upward. I stand taller and smile without realizing it. Concerns feel smaller and stress disappears. My predominant emotions during Sunday service are love, peace, openness, acceptance and joy. They run through me like streams of electricity. I feel bigger than usual, as if my body radiates outward.

Within that powerful space, surrounded by like-minded people and music, and messages that speak straight to my heart, I am changed and affected in a deep way that is difficult to put into words. I feel more my Self and more expansive. I am part of a great body of celebration, and also centered in myself and who I am. This is because when I am inside the great energy of my church, something within me *is* changed. I take in the vibration of that space, which is a very high vibration. In scientific terms, my own particles speed up as they're affected by the frequency of the particles around me; in metaphysical terms, I feel the presence of something greater than myself and am uplifted by its power.

The process can work in the other direction, too. Stuck at an airport on my way home from a speaking engagement, all flights delayed or canceled, the feeling in the air is tense and anxious whether I feel stressed or not. Sitting there as the hours creep by, surrounded by thousands of other harried travelers, it is difficult, sometimes impossible, to keep that energy from draining me. It is times such as this that I am so grateful that I understand these principles. It reminds me of the first lesson in managing my energy from the kind, small acupuncturist all those years ago. So I close my eyes and focus on my breathing, or make a point to make eye contact and smile with the strangers near me, perhaps striking up conversation to connect. I am aware of the energy around and within me and do all I can to keep my energetic consciousness high with the hope of both getting through it with greater ease, and bringing a sense of lightness to those near. I cannot always control what is happening around me, so my goal is to manage what is occurring within me. That is what I call managing my level of consciousness.

Your level of consciousness affects every single thing around you, everything you do, everything you feel, everything you create, everyone you encounter. Like attracts like on the energetic plane; this means that you attract other people, situations and relationships that vibrate at the same resonance as you. Just as your vibrating cells attract the chemicals that set off your psychosomatic reality, the vibration of your being attracts things, too.

If you live at a low average resonating level of consciousness, it is likely that you will attract low-resonance realities into your life (stressful circumstances, challenging relationships, employment difficulties and so on). Likewise, if you live at a high resonance, you will attract high-resonance realities (greater ease, supportive relationships and positive "coincidences"). When you incorporate higher, lighter, more beautiful thoughts, emotions, conversations and events into your day, your energy is lifted and you rise to a higher level of consciousness.

It is in understanding and managing your *energetic consciousness* rather than your time or stress that life mastery begins. As you recognize that it is your perception of any given event that creates your reaction to it, you can train yourself to shift your perceptions and create the experience of life that you desire. You must learn to feel your emotions and let them move through you. This is not about practicing denial or avoiding difficult emotions. It is about empowerment; recognizing that when you are psychologically healthy and well, you can consciously choose your experience of life. You can learn to practice the high-consciousness attribute of surrender moment-to-moment so that you do not suffer the ongoing effects of trying to be the master of the universe! You learn to release and let to, accepting what is happening around you and within you, and surrendering the rest to the greatness of Life itself.

Below is a graphic image to deepen your understanding. The center arrow in the spiral represents that we are always moving up and down these four levels of consciousness, and yet we all have one domain of consciousness where we most often experience and move through life. Bruce Schneider calls this one's "average resonating level of consciousness" or ARL. The colors on the graphic represent the energy centers of the body, known as the chakras, with the lower energies being at bottom of the spiral and the higher energies at the top.

Levels of Consciousness Application

My coaching client, Hank, was lamenting to me that his wife, June, had planned a vacation with a couple that he did not really enjoy. Mark and Sue were casual friends of Hank and his wife for many years. June and Sue were close friends, and Hank and Mark could enjoy a game of golf and chat here and there, but overall Hank did not really enjoy them. He felt they drank too heavily and that Mark was too controlling with their schedules and activities. I asked Hank what I ask most of my coaching clients, "What level of consciousness is that?" He was well versed in his use of this concept, so he just laughed and said, "Yeah, not the most powerful energy, huh?"

"What do you want to experience, Hank?" I asked him.

"Well, it's my vacation. I want to enjoy myself, I want to relax and not feel on the go all the time."

"Great! I can hear that. So what would it take for you to truly enjoy the time with your friends? How can you shift this?" I asked him.

"I could alter my negative perception of them for starters! They are great people. There is nothing wrong with them," he exclaimed.

"Yes, I will bet that will shift things! What if you take on getting to know them in a new and different way? What if you pay attention to them with an open mind and really try to engage? Do you think that might shift things?"

"Yes, I believe it would. I can do this. I just have to *be* different with them, and probably with my wife too!"

Hank went on to have a wonderful time on this trip. He got to know Mark in a different way. They even talked about Mark's drinking and Hank learned that Mark had been concerned about it too, but didn't know what to do. Mark brought it up over dinner with the four of them, and June offered to support Sue in drinking less when they went out together. It was a truly transformational time together. I asked Hank what he thought made the shift.

"I was being different with them. I didn't bring the energy that I was tolerating them. I wasn't being simply 'polite.' I was truly engaged and interested in getting to know them in a new way. That made all the difference. I even told Mark that I had been lamenting spending the vacation with them and he just laughed. He said he was shocked when Sue told him about the vacation plans because he never thought I would go for it!"

"Great job creating a different outcome, Hank. It is all about shifting consciousness. You did what it took to create a different experience for everyone, and it seems like it could be a profound difference at that!"

Change your consciousness and everything changes.

Chapter Twelve

Understanding Your Time Consciousness

The question of our relationship to time is both a mystery and a problem. The mystery of time has the power to quietly call us back to ourselves and to our essential humanness and freedom. The problem of time, on the other hand, agitates us and "lays waste our powers."

~Jacob Needleman, American philosopher and author of *Time and the Soul*

So how does this relate to your relationship with time? How does your level of consciousness impact your experience of chaos? You have a consciousness about everything and you most definitely have a consciousness about time! Remember earlier when I wrote about the question I have asked to thousands of seminar participants? "What do you most often say about time?" The predominant answer? "There's not enough of it!" Now that you have read this notion of levels of consciousness, let me ask you, what level of consciousness is "I don't have enough time"?

> *You have a consciousness about time!*

I'm sure you can quickly see that it is level one survival consciousness. The notion that there is not enough time (or money or love or anything else) is firmly rooted in L1C indicating that there is a scarcity of something, life is happening *to you* and you feel at a loss for what to do about it.

Here is a simple description of the levels of consciousness and your relationship with time.

Level 1: There's so much to do that I can't begin to keep up. I just don't have enough time to get everything done. It is too much. Days fly by and I don't even know what I'm doing most of the time. I try to stay on top of everything, but it is totally useless. I don't know why I bother trying.

Level 2: I get angry and frustrated when time gets away from me and I cannot get it all done. I work hard and do my best, but it is all just too much. I work harder than anyone I know, but it still seems that I can't get ahead. I have got to find ways to be more productive and get things done.

Level 3: I have the time I need for the things I want and need to do. As I increase my ability to make decisions that are aligned with what is important to me, I feel more and more empowered around time. I know that life is full of opportunities, but if I try to accomplish everything, I will never know inner peace. Therefore, I see time as a resource to be cherished rather than as a struggle to be won.

Level 4: Time is all there is because time is eternal. As I align my thoughts, beliefs and actions with this truth, my experience of time shifts according to my needs. I can use my energy to draw things to me more quickly or I can use my energy to slow things down. I am always experiencing the perfect flow of life; therefore I am always at peace.

We often don't acknowledge the truth that how we spend our time and our days is how we spend our lives. When we give up the notion that our lives exist as a potential "someday existence" we begin living with the truth that our *time* and our *life* are one and the same. Ask anyone who has been diagnosed with a terminal condition and they will tell you the preciousness that they come to feel toward time and life. But here is the hard truth: We are all terminal! We just don't live like we are. We live like we will never grow old, like our days are not numbered and like we have "forever and a day" to live our lives. Nothing could be further from the truth. Calming the chaos means that you recognize the sacredness of *this life here and now,* not living in the hope of life getting better "someday." It means being and doing the things that align with your highest sense of self, with your deepest desires and passions.

As you move through your day today, spend time reflecting on this notion. As you listen to others, ask yourself, "What level of consciousness is that conversation?" Then also, reflect on your own conversations and thoughts, and determine what level of consciousness you are bringing to each moment. There is no way to articulate the importance of this notion. Your consciousness gives you the quality of your life, so train yourself to notice and then shift into higher consciousness. It really is that simple. There may be times when you feel that it is just too hard to let go of the lower energies or emotions, when you want to move to a higher state, but you just can't. Perhaps you are too upset, or you are too committed to holding onto the anger or resentment or worry. It's okay. Allow those emotions to be there. If you simply surrender that you cannot shift right now, that alone will help you release and let go just a little. If you simply express the wish to move to higher consciousness, the energy of that thought (which is like a prayer) will help you soften and move higher. Try it and you will see!

Living life this way means that you are willing to consistently surrender being right for being peaceful, getting your way for establishing harmony. It is a radically different shift, but when you learn to do so (and you can) you will truly be managing your energy rather than your time and stress!

Section Four: It Is So Simple!
(But not easy!)

"Simple can be harder than complex: You have to work hard to get your thinking clean to make it simple. But it's worth it in the end because once you get there, you can move mountains."

~Steve Jobs, American innovator, founder of Apple computers

Chapter Thirteen

Managing Your Energy in Every Area of Life

Time is a finite resource. Energy is not.

~Tony Schwartz, business consultant, author

That brings us to another attribute of effectively managing your energy: a willingness to be *fully responsible* for how your life is going and how it is not. Your life will look radically different when you start generating it with clarity and intention rather than simply reacting to what is happening around you. It is a common, yet unhelpful, human characteristic to blame other people for the way things are; to think, feel and say that my struggles are because of my boss or the kids or I have too many hours to work or I have too many projects going on. There is a frequently expressed notion that life is happening *to me* (this reflects Level 1 Consciousness—L1C). In order to start managing your energy rather than your time, I invite you to live your life being fully responsible for the way your life looks and the way that it doesn't, and see how that impacts your choices. Can you begin making choices that support your energy rather than drain your energy?

To achieve the effectiveness and centered calm you desire, you need to increase your awareness of what is impacting your energy, both positively and negatively, and *then act according to this awareness.*

One of the tools I use to help determine to what degree you are managing your energy in increasingly effective ways is a simple self-assessment called the Energy Drain Inventory. This inventory looks at five areas of life and asks questions for you to see how and where you are unconsciously draining off life force energy through unhelpful, unproductive and unconscious behavior. Shifting your perspective to recognize that how you function in relation to your environment, wellbeing, self-management, relationships and finances largely determines the quality of your life is a powerful beginning to managing your energy.

Read each sentence and check off those that apply to how you are currently living your life. Not the way you *think you should be* living your life, but the actual current snapshot of your life. If a given item is usually the case, check it off. If an item is almost never present in your life, leave it blank.

Environment

☐ There is a lot of clutter around my home, car, garage, workplace and so forth.

☐ My work area and/or files are disorganized, cluttered or messy.

☐ I have stacks of mail, magazines or other paperwork that I do not manage.

☐ I often lose or misplace things.

☐ There are things in my home, in my car or at work that are in disrepair and needing attention (appliances that do not work properly, repairs that need to be made, painting that you want or need done, and so on).

Wellbeing

☐ I have some chronic condition (illness or pain, either physical or psychological) that I am not attending to (including addictions, anxiety, depression or innate fears).

☐ My eating and nutritional habits do not support my optimal health and well-being.

☐ I don't get enough rest or feel fatigued.

☐ My body is not at an ideal weight or fitness level and it bothers me or hinders me in some way.

☐ I often work long hours without taking adequate periods to rest and recharge.

Self-Management

☐ I procrastinate on daily tasks.

☐ I lose time in compulsive or addictive behavior (including internet surfing, email, TV, shopping, gambling, substances or video games).

☐ I have things I often think "I should be doing" but I am not taking action on.

☐ I often feel overwhelmed or over scheduled or am often late for appointments or meetings.

☐ I say "yes" to things (tasks, invitations) impulsively and later have second thoughts or regrets.

Finances

☐ I often worry about money, either daily budget or long-term savings.

☐ My bills are often late or overdue.

☐ I spend more than I earn, or have acquired a large amount of debt. Even if I do get a raise, it does not improve my financial situation.

☐ I pay little or no attention to my earning power, do not ask for raises or seek positions that would increase my financial bottom line.

☐ I do not feel adequately compensated for the work that I do.

Relationships

☐ I have difficulty letting go of upsets and sometimes blame others for my circumstances.

☐ I am often over-reactive emotionally—even if only with certain people.

☐ Many of my relationships, including at work, feel more draining than fulfilling.

☐ I am actively hiding something(s) from someone or perhaps several people.

☐ I lack the friendships, personal connections, love or support that I desire in my life.

Total
Score:

_____

_____

Energy Drain Inventory Scoring Tool

There are five categories, with five items each for a total of 25 items. Count the number of checks you have indicated on your inventory.

- 0-6: You manage your energy extremely well and are likely enjoying the full life benefits of such in peace of mind, vitality and wellbeing.
- 7-12: You manage your energy well but a few tweaks will go a long way toward increasing your overall wellbeing and satisfaction.
- 13-19: You are clearly struggling to manage your energy. Your focus is likely largely external, attending to too many people and/or commitments without adequate regard for your own wellbeing.
- 20-25: You are in serious jeopardy and are likely experiencing negative life outcomes such as sleep

disturbance, fatigue, restlessness, lack of focus and dissatisfaction with yourself and life.

I cannot say enough about the benefits of managing yourself around these twenty-five simple (but not easy) areas. So many people are drowning in their clutter, constantly stressed by overcommitting, being crushed under the weight of their debt. These factors, along with the others above, drain your life energy—and you are in charge of these. You can, over time, make shifts in each of these areas to increase your sense of self-empowerment and self-esteem that in turn raises your consciousness (and vice versa). All it requires is the awareness that how you live your life, the choices you make and the habits you develop impact the quality of your life, and then being willing to act accordingly.

Susan was a student in one of my programs who was intrigued with this notion that managing energy could in fact begin creating her life in the way that she wanted it to be. She was a successful business owner who, by most observable standards, had it all going for her.

Yet Susan was deeply unhappy with her life. She was grateful that her consulting business was going so well, but she felt lonely with very few close friends, no social communities that she enjoyed and no romantic relationship in her life. She began working the Energy Drain Inventory above, not completely convinced that clearing her clutter, changing her eating habits and showing up on time for things would bring friends and romance into her life.

Over a two-month period, she removed approximately two truckloads of things from her home, started preparing her food rather than constantly eating out (and dropped ten pounds as a side benefit), started managing herself in time in a way that had her be more prompt and less stressed getting places, and hired a contractor to take care of some long-standing repairs around her home. She started feeling better and feeling more optimistic about herself and her life.

During the course of the program she hooked up with another woman who was extremely socially active and engaged in a lot of community activities. They became fast friends around the coursework. They supported one another in raising their Energy Drain Inventory scores and then started going to shows, festivals, church and other activities together.

Through her increased social life, Susan almost forgot that she had set a goal of beginning to date and bring romance in her life. One afternoon as she was checking her email, she got a notification from an old dating site that she had not checked in quite some time. When she went to the site she saw a message from a new man who interested her quite a bit, despite the fact that he didn't fit her "ideal" profile.

They started exchanging messages, met up in a couple of weeks later, and never looked back. They moved in together after a few months and are slated to be married within the coming year.

I know this sounds "too good to be true." Many of the stories of people who learn to manage their energy rather than their time feel that way. The only way you will know for sure is, of course, to try it for yourself!

Chapter Fourteen

Managing the Energy of "Stuff"–
Clutter and Disorganization

Order is a very high consciousness principle.
Everything in the universe is supported and
sustained at the highest level through order.

~Jackie Woodside, the author of the book you're reading!

In my coaching work I support people in becoming aware of and dealing with what feeds and drains their energy. I call these things "Energy Boosters and Energy Busters." Energy Boosters are things that feed our sense of vitality, aliveness and satisfaction. Energy Busters are those things that drain and disempower us, even though we often continue to do them. By being aware of the things that we are doing (or not doing) and ways of being we have that contribute to our energy being drained, we can come to a greater sense of empowerment, making better choices in how we live and ultimately how we experience life.

In my work with thousands of people on this topic of energy busters, what fundamentally drains us come down to a few basic habits, which of course result from a few basic thought forms. The primary energy drains that I see time and again are disorganization and clutter. It is the "stuff" of our lives that often weighs us down and drains our sense of aliveness. The more stuff we have, the more there is for us to fix, tend to and organize. The less stuff we have, the lighter our environment and minds can be. This is completely contrary to our cultural notion of "he who dies with the most toys wins" but it is entirely true. The more stuff you have, the more you have to do. To be clear, I am not espousing shedding your possessions and going to live in a cabin like Thoreau at Walden Pond (although that can sound appealing at times, can it not?). I, too, own a fair amount of stuff. I own two homes, complete with two of everything needed to care for them; I have two cars, a boat, several bikes and five kayaks. I have an office outside of my home as well. And yet when people come into any of my environments, there is a near-constant observation that the space is so inviting, calming and very "Zen-like." People frequently remark, "This place has great energy!" That is because I understand what it means to *manage* energy. I have nothing in any of my environments that do not serve a purpose or touch my heart, mind and soul in some way. There is no clutter in my space (annoying, I know, but true!). I also live with (almost) no "emotional clutter," meaning my relationships are clean and free of upset or drama. When I sense that something is off in any of my relationships, I seek to get things cleaned up as soon as possible. That means being willing to be in communication, to listen, to apologize and to stay connected in a way that is meaningful and fulfilling. That is managing energy. Bringing the highest sense of care, attention and concern to all that you do and all that you own.

Clutter and disorganization weigh us down, make us less effective and often create negative self-talk ("What's wrong with me? I have to get a grip on this mess" and so on). You want to begin understanding clutter and disorganization from an *energetic perspective*. There is energy to everything. People have energy. Nature has energy. Everything is made up of molecules, and energy is created by the vibratory pattern of the molecules in motion. The more stuff that you have, the denser the energy in your environment becomes. In other words, it is harder to create the energetic conditions for changing your life, for creating the conditions that you want to bring forth. Change your energy, and change your life.

There is good research from the Princeton University Neuroscience Institute that relates directly to the importance of uncluttered and organized living. The study published in the January 2011 issue of *The Journal of Neuroscience* found that when your environment is cluttered, the chaos interferes with your ability to focus and decreases your brain's ability to process information. *Clutter creates mental distraction and decreases your ability to process information!*

The clutter around you competes for your attention much the way a car alarm going off distracts you when you are engaged in conversation over lunch. Even though you might be able to focus a little, you're still aware of the disturbing sounds around you. The annoyance also wears down your mental resources and you're more likely to become frustrated. I call clutter "mental noise." That is exactly how it feels to me when I am in a cluttered, disorganized environment; it just feels too "noisy."

This research shows that you will be less irritable, more productive, less distracted and able to process information better with an uncluttered and organized home and office.

I once worked with a coaching client by the name of Paul who was a preeminent author of several scientific textbooks. He had a contract with his publisher to get his next book out within the next few months and he was literally stopped; he could not get his thinking or his time organized. He kept saying it was because his technology was slowing him down, so he hired a friend of mine, who works as an in-home and small business technology consultant, to help him. After meeting with Paul a couple of times, my friend, who knows my work well since he was a graduate of my programs, referred him to me.

When I first met Paul, I was struck with what a brilliant mind he had, and yet, how incredibly anxious and disorganized he seemed to be. He really felt that, despite having published literally thousands of pages of written material, he would not be able to complete this next task. Within our first month of working together, I asked him what his work environment looked like and, as he described it to me, I was fairly certain about the root of his problem. Paul described three workstations set up in his tiny office, with piles of books and papers surrounding the floor and desks of each of these. He said he could only walk to each workstation through a small path on the floor that was clear of papers, boxes and books. I had him send some photographs of his office and it was worse than I had imagined. I can remember those images like it was yesterday. Boxes and piles of books and papers everywhere, empty coffee cups delicately balancing on top of piles, cleaning supplies tucked in an open slot between piles here and there, folders on top of papers on top of boxes on top of books. You get the picture.

I told Paul that I could help him get his book finished, but that he would need to stop trying to hammer out page after page of unsuccessful writing for at least a week. If he was willing to do so, I promised I could help him; otherwise, I offered to refer him to a different coach. He was frustrated and not particularly pleased, but he was also desperate so he accepted my offer. I gave him daily assignments to clear out the clutter in his office, starting one pile at a time, to get things filed, tossed out, sorted and organized by topic. He had to buy bookshelves and another filing cabinet to bring some semblance of order to his office, but after a solid week of work, the difference in his environment—and his mood— were astounding. He showed up in my office the following week looking sharper, more alive, more engaged than I had seen him look in the previous weeks. He had more bounce in his step and reported feeling enthusiastic about starting his writing project again. I gave him continued assignments to maintain the gains he had made.

Each evening, before he stopped writing, he had to organize his workspace for the next day. He could leave out books and articles that he was using for his current piece of writing, but everything else needed to be put away, including lunch and dinner plates, coffee cups and anything else that had made it to his workspace during the day. It was an astounding turnaround. He completed his book within the time frame his publisher had given him and felt proud of the piece he produced. He told me after the book came out that he completely thought I was nuts when I gave him those instructions and, if it weren't for how desperate he felt, he would have walked out of my office and not returned. Despite these rocky beginnings in coaching, Paul went on to become one of my biggest fans. He even started to teach his colleauges the importance of keeping your space organized so your mind can function in a more optimal fashion.

Chapter Fifteen

Clear Your Space,
Change your Life!

*Economics has nothing to do with satisfaction.
Everyone is the same. Wealth or affluence doesn't
alter fulfillment or quench a desire for happiness.
However, altering people's external settings to
satisfy and awaken their inner spirit
effects a kind of change.*

~Linda J. Parks, professional organizer and author of
Clear Your Space, Clear Your Mind

Clearing and organizing your space can impact other areas of your life as well, not just neurological functioning. I have worked with hundreds of people around decluttering and organizing their homes and workspaces and have truly seen miracles occur. I call this process the "back door approach" to transformation. You don't have to do all kinds of inner work to create change if you are willing to dig in and do the work of bringing order to your physical environment. However, to create the *sustained conditions for change,* both the inner and outer work are necessary.

I worked with a couple who had been experiencing financial difficulty. Donna and Eric understood and appreciated my energetic approach to creating change, so they hired me to help them clear any blocks they may have had that would block their inflow of money. I asked them to describe their physical environment to me—all of their home and workspaces, including the attic, basement and garage. They looked at each other and then at me somewhat sheepishly and admitted that each of these spaces was filled with years of family possessions that they had not cleared out for over 20 years. The next week they sent me pictures and I was shocked to see these spaces packed in near floor-to-ceiling with boxes and boxes of … well, of who knows what!

I worked with them over the course of a summer and fall to help them plan their approach, take action and stick with it. The first minor miracle occurred when they had two huge weekend garage sales that netted them over $1,500 in income. They were astounded to see so many of their old possessions bringing in cold cash! They continued their process, filling two dumpsters of old boxes of their kids' elementary school artwork, school papers and all sorts of things they had never let go. They gave a truckload of items to Goodwill—sheets, towels, clothing, kitchen supplies (they had about quadruple of every kitchen item you can imagine). They were definitely the type who held on to everything "in case they needed it someday."

Donna and Eric finished up this huge project sometime in the mid-fall, and what happened next was truly in the realm of miraculous. I kept telling them to stay open to the energy shifting, that something would happen to fill the energy void they had created, and that their financial life would improve because of their commitment, their work and the shifting energy. But even I could not imagine what happened next.

Donna had an older cousin who was a mildly mentally retarded man who was able to work and live independently in the community for all of his adult life. He lived a very modest existence, staying in the same small apartment for over 25 years, working at a local school as a custodian. He did not drive, and had no real social interests or hobbies apart from eating out in a few local places, watching TV and seeing his family. When he did not come to work one morning, the school called him, and when there was no answer, they assumed the worst since he never missed work. They called the police, who entered his apartment to find him dead in his bed. He had died peacefully in his sleep one night.

Donna and Eric had always looked after her cousin, so they were called to take care of his belongings and clean out his apartment. As they were doing so, they found two large black trash bags – the super-sized industrial type that he would have used at work. They were tucked away, one in his clothes closet, and another in the corner of his bedroom—and both were filled with cash! Donna and Eric were named executors of his estate, and soon learned that not only did he have over $50,000 in cash in his apartment, he had another $100,000 in his bank account. Given that his parents were deceased, and he had no siblings or children, Donna and Eric inherited the entire sum.

I know this story sounds like one of those too-good-to-be-true tales, but I promise you this is absolutely true. This is what can happen when you use your mental energy to set an intention, your emotional energy to commit to a new path in life and your physical energy to do the work of fulfilling on this new path; it is indeed creating the conditions for miracles!

You have got to begin dealing with how you are managing the energy of your space as well as the energy of your inner world of thought and emotion. Is the energy free-flowing, soft and malleable through the conscious use of order and clarity, or is your space heavy-laden and cramped due to an excess of things that have no use or meaning in your life? The energy of your consciousness is often mirrored by the energy of our physical surroundings. Your inner world will always be reflected back and mirrored to you by your outer world. At some point in your life, you

> *Your inner world will always be reflected back and mirrored to you by your outer world.*

have probably gone through a cleaning out and decluttering process, perhaps when you moved to a new home or apartment. How did it feel when you finally get that stuff out the door? It felt great, didn't it? There is an absolute correlation between moving the energy in your environment and elevating your mood. There is power and magic to consciously moving the energy in and around your life to enhance your highest good.

On the inventory below, there are two lists of items. One list reflects potential energy busters or drains. The other lists potential energy boosters, or things that feed your energy. Check off the items that frequently describe your experience in life. It does not have to be something that is present 100% of the time. But if the item can frequently be seen in your life, check it off.

At the end of the exercise, count up the number of energy busters you have and the number of energy boosters. You will quickly be able to see the degree to which you need to employ greater awareness toward your skills, habits, practices and ways of being in your life.

This inventory is designed to *raise your awareness* and help you determine the degree you experience energy drains that eventually lead to burnout, stress and fatigue and the degree you feel your energy is fed and enhanced, leading to a sense of empowerment, satisfaction and improved productivity and creativity.

ENERGY BUSTERS

☐ Over-committing	☑ Clutter
☐ Hoarding	☑ Disorganization
☑ Negativity and depression	☑ Resentment
☑ Need for external approval	☑ Comparing yourself to others
☑ Lack of clear, consistent planning	☐ Chronic hurry
☑ Inadequate sleep (not enough hours)	☑ Chaos
☑ Lack of meaning & purpose	☑ Being late
☐ Overspending	☑ Overeating
☑ Addictions of any kind	☑ Anxiety and worry
☑ Feeling victimized	☑ Chronically feeling overwhelmed
☐ Codependency (difficulty saying "no")	☑ Blaming others & yourself
☐ Defensiveness	☐ Poor diet & nutrition
☑ Excessive media (TV, texting, video games)	☐ Excessive noise
☐ Violence—directly or media	☑ Indecisiveness
☑ Feeling chronically stressed	☑ Lack of clarity & direction
☑ Financial insufficiency	☐ Illness or chronic pain

BOOSTERS

ENERGY BUSTERS

☐ Being optimized rather than stressed	☑ Nature
☑ Loving relationships	☑ Friends
☑ Fun & laughter	☐ Practicing mindfulness
☑ Slower pace	☐ Planning one's life and time
☐ Orderliness	☐ Peaceful surroundings
☑ Enjoying relaxation	☐ Sufficient rest
☐ Exercise & movement	☐ Setting meaningful goals
☐ Living your values	☐ Community/Belonging
☐ Doing things you enjoy	☐ Meaningful work
☐ Frequent positive thoughts	☐ Affirmations
☐ Meditation or stillness	☑ Healthful eating
☐ Expressing and feeling gratitude	☑ Practicing acceptance
☐ Setting and achieving realistic goals	☑ People who support you
☐ Balance	☐ Giving things away
☐ Prayer	☑ Spending time doing things you love
☐ Being productive	☑ Living within one's means
☑ Positive touch & hugs	☐ Optimism
TOTAL BUSTERS: _____	**TOTAL BOOSTERS:** _____

Now the next question is: of those things that are draining you, *to what degree* are they draining you? And does that make up for the amount that you're getting fed energetically? For example, let's talk about clutter and disorganization. They may be the only two items that you have on that whole list of energy busters, but your life is so cluttered and disorganized that you can't find anything, and you walk through your hallways with your hands at your sides. Your life is in a complete shambles because of it. Because the worksheet is just a quick look, you have to reflect on it and interpret how the busters and boosters are affecting you. You have to deal with *to what degree* a buster is draining your energy and *to what degree* a booster is lifting you up.

After completing this inventory, look to see whether you are experiencing more energy boosters or busters in your life. *From this inventory you can begin to chart actions to nurture your life energy.*

Energy Booster and Buster Action Plan

1. From the inventory above, I can see where I am draining precious life force energy, often unconsciously. The biggest energy busters in my life currently are:

Depression, anxiety, disorganized, lack of meaning & purpose

My action plan to reduce my energy busters is as follows; (For example: I will schedule one decluttering session per week for the next month to reduce the clutter in my home, I will make a decision about my career and inform my boss and co-workers within the next two weeks, I will establish a budget and spending plan this weekend and track my expenses, living within this budget for the rest of the year).

Declutter organize file cabinet, recycle or throw away items, Work on closet, pantry this weekend and everyweekend

2. From the inventory above, I can see where I can improve the ways I am feeding my precious life force energy. The energy boosters I will add or enhance are:

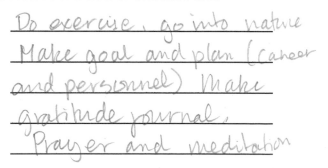

Do exercise, go into nature Make goal and plan (career and personnel) Make gratitude journal, Prayer and meditation

My action plan to add or enhance my energy boosters in my life is as follows (For example: I will spend time in nature once a week, I will join the lunchtime walking group at work, I will spend five minutes every morning in prayer before I start my day):

I will spend time in nature once a week, meet up with friend or talk once a week Do morning exercise, 5 min. meditation, and prayer, before bed time do gratitude journal. Go to bed at 10 wakeup at 6

Herein lies the core of my teaching: When we become aware of energy and begin to consciously design our lives to incorporate more of the higher, lighter, more peaceful energies and less of the low, stressful, chaotic energies, our cells literally begin to vibrate at a higher frequency, our personal energy changes. Higher frequencies are more malleable, easier to flow, easier to change; therefore, life itself gets easier.

It's that simple. But it's not that easy.

After going through this chapter, you will have developed a much greater awareness of your relationship to your energy. This is a crucial first step because you cannot change what you are unwilling or unable to see.

Section Five: The Power of Focus

One reason so few of us achieve what we truly want is that we never direct our focus; we never concentrate our power. Most people dabble their way through life, never deciding to master anything in particular.

~Tony Robbins, author, empowerment speaker, businessman

Chapter Sixteen

Busy Versus Productive

Beware the barrenness of a busy life.

~Socrates

Do you tire of hearing people's stories of how busy they are as much as I do? Being busy serves so many purposes that deserve deeper exploration. So many people literally spend their lives being busy to avoid delivering on *Who They Really Are* and what they came here to deliver. They are busy doing good things, but they keep themselves in constant motion, constantly pursuing or attending to the next thing, yet not realizing they are avoiding what they are really here to express in the world. Following your heart and pursuing your true calling takes tremendous courage. It requires a willingness to go against the grain of what our cultural norms tell us we are "supposed to be doing" with our grown-up lives. There is tremendous vulnerability in stepping into one's calling or purpose when it requires redesigning your life. But there is also tremendous freedom and power to it.

> *So many people literally spend their lives being busy to avoid delivering who they really are and what they came here to be.*

121

There are ways of being responsible in responding to one's calling. But you're going to have to address the degree to which you are keeping yourself busy so that you are not productive on what really matters to you! You need to address even further, in your heart, what lies underneath that busyness: the fear, the vulnerability, the what-ifs and the unknown.

So my question is, "You are busy, but are you creating what you desire in your life?" There is a tremendous distinction between being busy and productive, two words that reflect similar notions, but are energetically wildly divergent. How do you feel when you say you are "so busy" or you hear others say this to you? What is the energy of that word? Most often, when I ask people that question, the reply is that "busy" feels chaotic, frantic, disorganized, pressured. Being busy means that we are always engaged in activity, moving quickly from one thing to another, but never really certain what is getting done or producing clear outcomes. People who report that they are chronically busy most often say that they start on many things, but finish very little.

I use the notion of being productive in a whole different way. Stop for a moment and reflect on how that word feels to you. When you say you felt productive today, how do you feel? What is the energy of that word? Productive indicates that things are actually getting accomplished, that there is clarity and order to the activity of the day, there is a sense of greater focus. My definition of productive is that you are *clearly and consistently taking ground on what is important to you, producing an intended outcome that you desire and for which you find meaning.*

"Busy" means always being engaged in activity, and very often they are activities that do not feed us or that we do not find meaningful. Now that doesn't mean that all of the activity is meaningless, but the *feeling of* being chronically busy is endless engagement in activity and it is draining. The feeling of productivity is moving forward with clarity to produce a desired outcome, and it feeds, stimulates and nourishes the mind and soul.

Preeminent psychologist and researcher Nathanial Braden described the link between productivity and self-esteem in his book, *The Psychology of Self-Esteem*. Braden showed that the better you feel about yourself, the more productive you are and the more productive you are, the better you feel about yourself. It is an ongoing cycle of positive energy in your life.

Let's break these concepts down a little more for you so you can begin identifying the skills, habits and ways of being that you have been practicing regarding busy behavior versus productive behavior. Yes, that is right, we actually PRACTICE certain behaviors over time until they become unconscious ways of being or habits! You might not think of it in this way, but you have truly practiced your busyness behavior, albeit unconsciously, for many years.

To begin discerning this more deeply, I use a very distinct set of characteristics for each of these two principles to help people identify which behaviors support and feed their energy versus drain their energy. Here is a grid that you can use to assess your own busyness versus productivity skills:

BUSY	PRODUCTIVE
☐ Scattered	☐ Intentional
☐ Disorganized	☐ Orderly
☐ Random	☐ Planned
☐ Reactive	☐ Responsive
☐ Stressed	☐ Optimized
☐ Chaotic	☐ Centered
☐ Overwhelmed	☐ Enthusiastic/ Inspired
☐ Time as enemy	☐ Time as opportunity
☐ Driven	☐ Focused
☐ Anxious	☐ At ease
☐ Confused	☐ Clear

Let's look at each of these pairs in detail.

Scattered vs. Intentional: Busyness tends to go hand in hand with being scattered and unclear about what actions to take, how to move forward with clear progress on things that you care about. There is a tendency to do a little of this, a little of that, but bringing very little to a state of completion and satisfaction. Intentional, on the other hand, reflects a tendency to move forward through the day with a sense of clear purpose for what needs to be accomplished and a clear plan on how to accomplish it.

Disorganized vs. Orderly: Disorganization is a hallmark trait of people who get caught up in the busyness chaos. While many people lament that they wish they were more organized, very few recognize that what needs to change in order for their organization to improve is their mental clarity, or mental order!

It is impossible to lead an organized life without first organizing your mind. Yes, it is true that a disorganized mind creates a disorganized life! Mail piles up, bills get overlooked; and keys, wallets, hats, gloves, cleats and baseball gloves get lost (frequently!). Shifting behavior from disorganized to orderly brings a whole new energy to the feeling of your day, and yes, even to your life. I know it may *feel like* that shift is impossible, but the truth is that you are just not yet trained in how to move through your days in an orderly fashion.

> *A disorganized mind creates a disorganized life!*

Order is a very high consciousness principle. Look around and you will see that the entire universe operates in intricate order. One season follows the other, the tides ebb and flow with exact precision, nature unfolds with effortless ease as it follows the universal experience of an orderly universe. When you tap into that same energy, bringing order to the living of your life, you will begin to function with the same level of consistency, clarity, predictability and ease as you see all around you in nature.

Random vs. Planned: Moving through life in a random fashion is one of the characteristics of leading a life that lacks a sense of meaning and purpose. A lot of people say that they like to "go with the flow" rather than plan out their days and their lives. That is fine if you don't want to get everything that you can from life, and give everything you can to life. But very few people can create an extraordinary life without planning. Take Michelangelo's painting of the Sistine Chapel, for example. I think most people would agree that this work of art represents an extraordinary feat. Such an exemplary piece of work did not occur by "going with the flow." In fact, Michelangelo spent almost as long *planning the work* as he did completing the actual painting of it.

He first had to determine what painting style to use for the ceilings that were going to be viewed from 60 feet below. Once he determined that the painting method known as *buon fresco* would be most appropriate to the task, he then had to learn how to paint in this method—and it was known as the most challenging painting method of the era, used only by master painters. There is a complete parallel here to your life. You can live your life by the "go with the flow" philosophy;

anyone can do that. But it requires mastery to live your life with a clear plan, purpose and intention and then move in the direction you intend. Your life can be a masterpiece, your own work of art with your own indelible signature!

This notion of planning one's life is often met with fierce resistance from spiritual people who say they only want to do God's will and follow God's plan. I couldn't agree more, which is why I say that planning versus living randomly is so crucial! One of my highest values is to live my life in alignment with my highest potential and purpose, which is a very spiritual process; but that does not mean that once I catch a glimpse of God's plan for me, I sit back and wait for every little detail to come my way! To me, that is both spiritually and ontologically lazy! (Ontological laziness is being lazy in managing yourself and your being). Getting clear on your calling is crucial, and from there, start to plan what you will do to "help God out" bringing that plan into manifestation. You are, after all, a human being on the earth plane and, given this fact, I believe you are called to be in action, in a planned way, toward what is yours to do.

Reactive vs. responsive: Living in chronic chaos robs you of your ability to move thoughtfully through your day, responding rather than reacting to each new or unexpected turn. Reactivity is the hallmark of chaos in which you lose your ability to consciously choose how you will respond to events and circumstances. Reactivity is great in a fight-or-flight, high-adrenalin moment; you want to be able to move quickly if your child is dashing off toward the edge of the road. But operating in constant fight or flight not only exhausts you, it reduces your ability to see the bigger picture and move forward with thoughtful attention. Fight-or-flight reactivity is geared for laser focus, not for holding the fullness of the masterpiece of your life. As you move from busy to productive, you can truly begin to "see the forest for the trees" as life events occur, and then you can consciously choose to dance with the rhythm of your life, rather than spinning along on the wheel of endless to-do's.

Stressed vs. optimized: You may forget that stress is not something that you catch like a cold, but it results from your response to the outer circumstances of your life. Not all stress is bad stress. The right levels of stress response, such as heightened adrenalin before giving a speech or a sales presentation will help you to optimize your skills and deliver on a higher level than if you are overly stressed (panicked, frightened, overwhelmed) or if you are operating suboptimally (bored, unfocused, tangential). Being optimized means you are challenged to the level appropriate to your skills and interests—neither bored nor overwhelmed. Stressed means that you are operating on high adrenalin, which leads to burnout and fatigue.

Chaotic vs. centered: So much of how you are moving through your day is filled with a sense of chaos, barely getting from one thing to the next, moving into the next activity mentally before you have finished the one you are engaged in now, going non-stop to take care of the home, the kids and the job. In chaos, there is no room to breathe, let alone integrate, think and feel. Living centered means that you live in the present moment, allow yourself spaces to breathe, to check in with yourself (and even with your kids and your spouse) before rushing into the next activity. It means bringing mindful awareness to doing what you are doing in any given moment.

I remember a time when my spouse had an injury and could not walk or drive for several months. I was going non-stop from morning to night, getting our son to and from school (an hour away from our home), running errands, preparing meals, doing household chores and running my business on top of everything else. (My respect for single parents was once again confirmed!) I realized if I spent the entire time worrying about the next thing I had to do, these next several months would be brutally difficult on me. So I shifted my focus from the long list of things I needed to get done, to *each individual moment*. And what I found was that in each individual moment, I was absolutely fine. I could enjoy driving my son to and from school. I could rest while doing the food shopping–rest my mind if not my body. The entire experience shifted as my focus changed. Once I got centered and present in each moment, I was able to move through the long litany of activities in a much more relaxed and even restful fashion.

Overwhelmed vs. Enthusiastic/Inspired: I once gave a talk to about 300 military personnel. It was an amazing feeling to stand before this large gathering of men and women in full military attire, sitting bolt upright, with keen attention. I was speaking to them about leadership, and began the talk asking them what they wanted to get out of the lecture. One of the men in the back of the room said he wanted to know how to inspire people. I told him that the best way to inspire others is to live a life that you are inspired by. If I am inspired by my own life, by my character, my integrity, my goals, my mission and the life I am leading, I absolutely believe that others will see my inspiration and enthusiasm and will be inspired as well. But how do you lead an inspired life if you're walking around feeling frazzled and overwhelmed 90 percent of the time? I don't think it is possible.

> *Time is not the problem; your relationship to time is the problem.*

Have you ever noticed that almost nothing is fun when you are living in "overwhelm"? Even things that you normally enjoy can feel like "just one more thing to do." That experience is far too common today and it is no way to live. It is, in fact, not living as much as it is surviving. And life is not something to be survived. Shifting your skills and ways of being from busyness toward productivity (and this book will teach you how to do so) will allow you to get out of the overwhelm that literally sucks the life out of you, and move you toward leading a life of inspiration.

Time as enemy vs. time as opportunity: You will not shift out of chronic chaos without shifting this paradigm—from seeing time as your enemy to seeing time as merely opportunity. Time as your enemy means that you are constantly fighting time, feeling a scarcity of time and feeling that time is against you. While there is a great deal of cultural consensus around this notion, it is not a truth.

The truth is that time simply is. It is an indiscriminate resource that we all have the same access to. Time is not the problem; your relationship with time is the problem. As we already saw in the previous section, your relationship with time lives inside your ongoing level of consciousness. Shift your relationship to time and watch your life experience change. Referencing philosopher Jacob Needleman again, "Our relationship to time is what it is because we lie to ourselves about what we are and what we can do and we hide from ourselves what we are meant to be." (*Time and the Soul*, 2003).

I always say, "I have all the time I need for what is mine to do!" That does not mean that I am sitting around with nothing to do. I am running my business, playing sports, going to board meetings, taking care of my home and child and marriage just like everyone else. What it means is that I locate all of my activities within a sphere of meaning regarding *Who I Am* and who I came here to be. By this I mean that my life has a larger purpose and that all of my activities are geared toward that greater purpose of growth in consciousness and my soul's expression.

I am committed to living in "high time-consciousness." I create the beliefs I want to experience about time rather than unconsciously absorbing the mass consciousness around me. And so can you!

Driven vs. Focused: Prior to my visit to the sweet acupuncturist who told me I was not going to live very long if I didn't change my ways, I was the picture of someone who was living in level two consciousness (L2C): driven, frantic, always pushing and working harder. I had a model work ethic. I strove to do everything well. Even the things I did for fun had a driven quality to them—late nights, competitive sports and a pace that would put even the most committed overachievers to shame. While many people may look at my life today and say the same elements are there, the difference is *qualitative*. I do things now being focused rather than driven. Being driven involves forcing an outcome rather than allowing things to flow. It is an "If it is going to be, it is up to me" mindset.

When you are *driven*, there is a pressured sense that does not let you rest. *Focus*, on the other hand, sees a clear path toward an end. There is action to take and commitments to be maintained toward that end. But there is not the pressured attachment of having to make things go a particular way. There is a sense of freedom, ease and expansiveness in being focused on an outcome that is important and meaningful.

Unfortunately, there is an incredible loss of the ability to focus in our culture as a result of the onslaught of media and information coming our way. I find it particularly amusing that as I was writing this section of the book I went to the Internet for reference material and each time I took my computer screen out of "non-distraction mode" (love that function!), I found myself reading the emails that popped up in the tiny window on the top right of my screen, then following the link in the email I received, then responding to the email, only to subsequently forget what I was writing about! Sound familiar? The more we lose our ability to focus, the more we feel driven. When you lose the ability to think deeply and sustain thinking over time, the less you feel alive, vital and engaged.

Anxious vs. at ease: Anxiety disorders are the most common mental conditions in our culture, with 18% of the population impacted by some form of anxiety (Anxiety and Depression Association of America). It is hard to relax when you feel busy all the time. (Not that you haven't noticed that!). But which came first? Did we first become an anxious culture or did we get busy to quell our anxiety? It is an interesting question and one that deserves further inquiry. For now, though, let's just look at the need to move from our sense of anxiety (L2C) to being at ease with life, time and the circumstances that come our way (mid to high L3C). (We will get into the "how to" shortly).

Confused vs. clear: You can see that as these qualities of being busy add up, they can lead to major mental confusion. Chronically reacting to what is coming at you instead of choosing to respond to life events, being driven by anxious fears and worries about getting it all done and keeping it all straight in your head, over-committing and being in constant motion all take their toll on your mental clarity. These elements lead to forgetfulness, mindless errors, distraction and an overall lowered sense of self-esteem. Confusion is the name of the game when our neurology can't keep up with our technology, and that is primarily what we are living with now.

So the key question for you is, "Which are you, busy or productive?" I have asked that question to thousands of course participants over the last ten years and, across the board, people point to the fact that they are feeling and operating as busy instead of productive. It is one of the ailments of our culture, but it is an undiagnosed condition!

It's time to tell the truth; the way we are living and working is not working any longer. Our technology has outpaced our neurology and we are overwhelmed, overloaded and living in chaos.

Perhaps the worst part of this scenario is that people are afraid to talk about this in any meaningful way. Assumptions all around us seem to say that busy is cool or hip or something that defines our sense of worth and success. Brigid Schulte writes in her book, *Overwhelmed: Work, Love and Play When No One has Time*, that there is a new cultural subtext going on and it is the "busier than thou" mentality. Everyone is crazy, busy, nuts and it is time to start questioning what is driving our minds and our lives.

One way to begin doing so is to take on a little experiment with the people in your life. In your day-to-day interactions in the coming days, have conversations with different people about this distinction between busy and productive and what you are noticing about yourself.

For example, you say to your coworker, "Hey, how are you doing today?" They will very likely say some variation of, "Oh, my gosh. I am so busy."

You say, "You know, I've just been thinking about that. Since everybody is always busy, I'm really trying to learn how to be more productive." Then take the time to tell them the distinction you are working with that was presented in the preceding pages. See what they say or if they can even attend to what you are saying!

I suggest you to do this exercise for two reasons: 1) so that you more deeply integrate these concepts and this distinction between busy and productive; 2) if there is something you want and need to learn, the best way to learn it is to teach it to someone else.

Another thing I would like to invite you to take on this week is how you respond when people reference you being busy. I get asked to do a lot of things, and the requests always start with "Jackie, I know you're busy, but would you..." I respond with, "I'm never busy, always productive." I do this because I want to constantly infuse my thoughts and my consciousness with the notion that time is merely a resource that I have and it is up to me how I use it *and how I feel about it.* I do not want to be unconsciously absorbed into the mainstream default culture that says we are all busy, frantic and living in chaos. I am never busy, always productive.

> *"I'm never busy, always productive."*

Section **Six:** Living Your Life in Alignment

Unless what you are doing on a daily basis reflects your most deeply held values, you will never experience inner peace.

~Hyrum Smith, author and creator of the
Franklin Day Planner

Chapter Seventeen

Measure in Meaning

It is only with the heart that one can see rightly.
What is essential is invisible to the eye.

~Antoine de Saint Exupéry, from
The Little Prince

Leadership and management icon, Peter Drucker, identifies knowing your values as one of the top qualities of great achievers (*Harvard Business Review*, 2010). So often we feel like our lives are passing and we get so caught up in all that we are doing that we scarcely notice. Time seems to be accelerating and there is an odd sense that we barely experience our lives. In my coaching work and in my work as a therapist, I have found over and over again that people feel a great deal of stress because they are busy doing things they feel they "have to do" rather than things they say they long to do. It is appropriate to question whether or not your whole life is passing by without you. This feels to be more and more the case when meaningful time, intention and connection disappear from how you are creating and living your life.

There is less and less to remind us what it means to be a human *being*, rather than a human *doing*. There is very little support for crafting one's life according to one's own heart and soul, rather than following the whims of the prevailing culture. Take for example the plight of Eric and Charlotte Kaufman, who in April 2014, decided to sail around the world with their two babies and ended up in perilous straits, needing to be rescued by emergency personnel as one of the children was sick and their boat was in serious disrepair.

While many questioned their judgment, the Kaufmans are an example of people bucking societal mores and seriously paying the price. They were loudly ridiculed for being negligent, stupid and insane to take on such an ambitious adventure with their two small children. They bucked what society says is right, normal or even moral. Yet, from their perspective, they were living the life of their dreams. For avid sailors who lived on their boat, they did not see engaging in such a trip as being outrageous given the way they value life at sea.

While the Kaufmans may be an extreme example, living in alignment means bringing cohesion to your life—aligning your choices, actions, behavior, conversations and ways of being with your values, dreams and desires. In order to do that you must first know what you value and what you want.

Claire was a coaching client of mine for a relatively short time. She entered into one of my coaching programs saying that she had wanted to take one for years, but had been too afraid to do so. She said that she knew that enrolling in my programs would "force her" to do what she had been avoiding for many years—leaving her secure, well-paying corporate sales job, which she said she hated, to pursue teaching yoga and doing wellness coaching.

Claire's story is not unique or unfamiliar to me as a coach (or as a therapist for that matter). I hear it all the time from people feeling that they are in a default life that they did not intend to create, and now that they are so far down the road, they don't know how to get themselves out of it. This is truly one of the most difficult types of chaos–feeling trapped in making a living rather than designing a life.

Claire worked in my program for about six months and was tenacious in her willingness to make change. Within the first three months, she gave her resignation to her boss and worked out a comfortable severance package that would afford her several months to get her new business at least somewhat underway. Despite her significant fear and anxiety of giving up a hefty six-figure salary, she went through with her resignation and spent a few months sorting out what to do next. She realized that the values she wanted to express more fully had to do with wellness, excellence and peacefulness. She started teaching yoga and doing wellness coaching within a few months of leaving her job, but after several months, she found that she missed the teamwork, stimulation and collaboration of her corporate work, just not the frantic pace.

Continuing to hone in and clarify her values and what she wanted to experience, Claire started looking at doing corporate coaching and training work, where she could in fact blend her values of wellness, teamwork, excellence and stimulation, but not recreate the frenzy, chaos and meaninglessness of her former sales role. She said that this one simple exercise of *aligning her choices and behavior with what she truly valued* and wanted to experience in life saved her life. Maybe not her literal, physical life, but it saved her life in the sense of her life force energy, and sense of meaning and satisfaction.

Values Clarification Exercise

In order to get more engaged in what is important to you, you must first discern what that is! What is it that you love, that you want your life to be about, that you want to be known for? What do you want your legacy to be? These are big questions, and I believe the answers to them truly have the potential to begin "right-siding" your life, pointing you toward experiencing and expressing the deeper nature of who you are and what you came here to this life to be— exactly like Claire experienced in the example above.

It is truly striking to me how few people can actually answer these questions right away. So much of what we come to think or believe in our lives is simply inherited from our family, education or religious background, or received by osmosis from our prevailing culture. It is ironic that Americans pride themselves on individualism and yet can scarcely answer this question: what do you truly value, what do you want your life to be about?

I am not talking about the values of your church, your parents, your socioeconomic level, your colleagues or your peers. I am talking about you—what I call the "You of you." This is the part of you that you think about but perhaps are afraid to talk about or take action on for fear of being ridiculed or met with disapproval. Things like my client Claire wanting to leave a high-paying job to teach yoga and do wellness work, or one of my colleagues, Joy, who left a successful law practice to become a minister. These longings get far too little attention in our hectic, gotta-get-it-all-done days.

I want to guide you in doing the work of discerning your core values. There is no right way to do this, but I have found over the years that having some kind of a guided process helps to stimulate thinking and get the creative juices flowing. Below are some questions that can guide you as you begin this discernment process. This exercise provides the grounding to know how to align your actions and your day-to-day activities so that you begin, slowly at first, to craft your life more from the inside out for what rings true in your heart and soul.

1. Identify five to seven people whom you admire, who have touched your life in a positive way, whom you would like to be like. These people can be living or dead, known to you or those you have never met. List them here:

Wayne Deyer, 1820 eh,
Elizabeth Gilbert Anita Morgani

2. Write down the qualities and characteristics you most admire in each of these people. (List at least one for each person above, or list more if applicable.) For example, if you listed Gandhi as a person you respect, what was it about him that you admire: his clarity of commitment, his

accomplishments, or his commitment to non-violence? For each person above, identify what about these individuals truly touches and inspires you.

kindness   insight   teacher
honesty   walk the talk generosity
action   knowing   conscious

3. Write down the five qualities or characteristics you most appreciate about yourself. If you cannot think of any, write down what others have told you they appreciate about you. In other words, what are your core strengths?

seeker   sincere
positive   trying to be best
conscious

4. What topics or issues do you get very passionate about? List 8-10 topics here:

spirituality, life experience,
food/cooking, great place to visit
mystery of world/universe
sustainable living, simplicity,
space clearing, beauty, aliveness
worthy

_____

_____

_____

_____

_____

5. Looking at the lists above, do you notice areas of repetition? Do you see things that you admire in others that you also have as qualities within yourself or as issues that you are passionate about? These qualities or issues are likely some of your more prized values. Choose five of them and write the themes here:

Conscious, observative, humble
humor, kind, worthiness, honest

_____

_____

_____

_____

_____

These five qualities will help you see what lies at the heart of your core values.

To continue this discernment process, I also use a simple checklist to help generate your thinking. To help you further discern your unique, personal values that you want to align your energy and resources with, select *only 5* values below to be identified as your core values. Place a check in

145

the box next to the value. Remember that each item listed below is a valuable quality, attribute or skill, so of course you value all of these. But the question for you to discern is which five of these values most speak to you, resonate with whom you are and what you want to create and express in your life.

Choose five here:

☐ Achievement/Accomplishment   ☐ Adventure

☑ Alignment/Living Your Values   ☐ Art

☑ Authenticity   ☐ Autonomy

☑ Beauty and Aesthetics   ☐ Belonging/ Community

☐ Collaboration   ☐ Contribution/ Service

☐ Commitment   ☐ Communication Skills

☐ Earning Power (financial)   ☑ Empowerment

☐ Enjoyment/Fun   ☐ Entertainment (TV,theatre,etc).)

☐ Environmental Sustainability   ☐ Excellence/Mastery

☐ Family   ☐ Financial Independence

☐ Fine Foods   ☐ Freedom

☐ Generosity   ☐ Gratitude

☐ Growth and Learning   ☐ Health, Wellness, Fitness

☐ Honesty   ☐ Humor

- [ ] Integrity/ Being Your Word
- [ ] Knowledge
- [x] Loving/kindness
- [ ] Meditation/Mindful Living
- [ ] Order/Organization
- [ ] Planning
- [ ] Prayer
- [ ] Recognition
- [ ] Risk-taking
- [ ] Science/Exploration
- [x] Self-Expression
- [ ] Solitude
- [x] Spiritual Growth
- [ ] Tradition
- [ ] Transformation
- [ ] Vitality/Zeal
- [ ] Other:

- [ ] Justice
- [ ] Leadership
- [ ] Loyalty
- [ ] Nurturing
- [x] Peace and Tranquility
- [ ] Playfulness
- [ ] Personal Power
- [ ] Results
- [ ] Romance and/or Intimacy
- [ ] Security
- [ ] Service to others
- [ ] Success
- [ ] Spontaneity
- [ ] Transcendence
- [ ] Travel
- [ ] Wealth

_____

_____

_____

Values Clarification Completion

Compare the two lists from the two previous exercises here:

_____	_____
_____	_____
_____	_____
_____	_____
_____	_____

What do you see? What similarities are expressed or what themes emerged?

From the two lists above, choose five of these items and establish these as your core values!

MY FIVE CORE VALUES ARE:

alignment / Living your value

self expression

peace & beauty

worthiness & kindness

empowerment

Establishing your core values is an important step to calming the chaos because until you discern what is truly important to you, you will not be able to truly craft your days and your life to experience those most important elements. Doing so is a central part in managing your energy rather than your time. The next section of this book deals with just that— how to actually manage yourself in time in such a way that you feel deeply connected to what matters to you, aligned with your values, and yet in a manner that maintains sanity rather than adding to the chaos all around you. That, as you are about to see, requires a fair amount of planning and intention.

Section Seven: Planning and Intention

This is the true joy of life, the being used for a purpose recognized by yourself as a mighty one; being a force of nature instead of a feverish, selfish little clod of ailments and grievances, complaining that the world will not devote itself to making you happy.

I am of the opinion that my life belongs to the community, and as long as I live, it is my privilege to do for it whatever I can. I want to be thoroughly used up when I die, for the harder I work, the more I live.

Life is no "brief candle" to me. It is a sort of splendid torch which I have got hold of for a moment, and I want to make it burn as brightly as possible before handing it on to future generations.

~George Bernard Shaw,
American playwright

Chapter Eighteen

Self-Management is the Key

*"How often do you feel overwhelmed by the
demands you place on yourself and those placed on
you by your friends, co-workers and life in general?
The real problem is not everything that is being
asked of you but forgetting that you have the power
to choose how you will respond to everything that's
being asked of you. Claiming your ability to choose
is the dynamic difference between your feeling
pushed and pulled around all the time and
intentionally living–sometimes dancing even–to the
rhythm of holy empowerment. That brings us to the
fundamental question:
Who is in charge of your life?"*

~Dr. Kirk Byron Jones, author of *Addicted to Hurry*

In this section, we are going to start dealing with the practical, "earth plane" structures and strategies that will help you to be the least stressed, most productive person you know. The "least stressed" part of that statement relates to the previous sections. You can see that as you align your activities with what you value, your sense of meaninglessness will diminish. As you shift your level of consciousness from the lower levels of victimization, apathy, anger and blame to the higher levels of purpose, possibility and joy, your life takes on a whole different energy–you literally feel better.

153

But if you do all of this and do not address your practical skills and habits with regard to getting things done, you still will not be operating in an optimized, exciting and fulfilling way. So we are going to address the practical skills, habits and strategies that will create you as being the most effective person you know!

As you can probably intuit from what I have said so far, it requires commitment to develop these kinds of skills, habits and practices. That is why we spent the first part of this book creating the "compelling why" for doing the hard work of developing better productivity and effectiveness skills. What is it that you want to experience and express in life? What do you want to bring to life? That is your compelling why, and it has to be truly compelling for you because *it is easier to live in the lower energies*. It's true! It is easier and takes less energy to live a life where you take little or no responsibility for the way things are in your life, where you blame other people for your circumstances and rely on the assistance of others rather than doing the work of transforming yourself to lead an empowered life. It is easier, yes, but it is way less fun and fulfilling! In fact, it is fairly miserable to live this way!

Shifting your life from miserable, to ordinary, to extraordinary takes tremendous commitment, and therefore having a clear, compelling "why" is part of what will drive you to stay the course. Take a moment now to go back to the beginning of the book and review what you wrote that you wanted to experience or create as a result of doing the work of calming the chaos. Allow the energy of that vision to fill your mind and heart again so that you stay committed to the work of transforming your life from chaos to calm!

You are not disorganized, bad, less than or a loser in any way. There is nothing "wrong with you." You are just not well trained in systematically bringing your goals and dreams into fruition. That is about to change. But you cannot even begin thinking about living in this higher way—being the ongoing creator of your dreams—until you first calm the chaos of your life. This section will provide you with everything you need to do just that. But remember once again, knowledge does not produce change! *Knowledge applied produces change* (yes, you have read that before in this book!) Just reading this book and setting it aside will make no difference in your life.

The Neurology of Overwhelm and Chaos

In order to increase your productivity and get out of the frantic cycle of chaos, you need to understand what is causing the chaos in the first place. We are living in the information age. One of the things I often say about that is that our neurology has not kept pace with our technology. We are simply not yet neurologically evolved enough to keep up with the pace of the information overload we are living with. This is not something that is going to change anytime soon as the rate of information being generated in our world is astronomical. Check out these facts:

- Ninety percent of the world's data, for all time, was generated over the last two years (*Science Daily*, May 2013)

This one is totally mind-bending to me:

- In 2010, Eric Schmidt, then Google CEO, reported that every two days we create as much information as we did up to 2003! That's right — every two days we generate as much information as since the dawn of mankind up until the year 2003. And that data was from three years ago! Can you imagine the current rate?

The point here is that our brains simply cannot process the amount of information coming at us, let alone the near-constant stimulation of having one device with us all the time that allows us to take pictures, watch videos, pay bills, surf the Internet, update our Facebook status, apply for a job, talk to a friend (Huh? Does anyone use the telephone function any longer?), get a date, find an apartment, book a flight and a host of other activities–almost everything but do the laundry and walk the dog–all constantly at our fingertips!

Think of it this way: imagine that your brain is like one of those clear glass fishbowls, and your thoughts are like ping pong balls. There is only so much room to fit in so many balls before they spill all over the floor! The same is true of our thoughts. We have only so much mental real estate at our disposal before we start operating under the influence of Information Fatigue Syndrome. Yes, that is correct, there is even a clinical syndrome identified that far too many of us fit into. While it is not yet a clinical diagnosis recognized by the Diagnostic and Statistical Manual (DSM) in the field of psychiatry, Information Fatigue Syndrome is a stress-related disorder that was identified and coined by British psychologist Dr. David Lewis. It includes symptoms such as:

- Poor concentration

- Sleeplessness

- Hurry sickness (the unending feeling of needing to rush or feeling pressured)

- Chronic irritability

- Increased stress and anxiety

- Compulsive "plugged in" behavior

- Depression

- Feeling burned out

Sound familiar, anyone? We are constantly plugged in but so rarely connected. This leads to an overwhelming sense of anxious preoccupation with what we need to do next.

The remedy comes through applying the principles I spoke of above, bringing order, which is a very high-consciousness principle to living of your daily life. To calm the chaos in your outer world, you must first calm the chaos in your inner world by bringing planning and intention to your life.

Planning is a linear process that brings order to the day-to-day activities of your life. Planning moves you away from busyness toward the order and intentionality of productivity. But let me ask you something. How much time do you spend *doing* the activities of your days? You will probably answer somewhere in the realm of 14-16 hours per day. And how

157

much time do you spend *planning* those activities? I don't mean thinking "I've got to get this done" or mulling over your day while you are in the shower. I mean sitting down with your schedule and determining what you want and need to do and when you are doing to do it.

Planning and intention hold very different energies and represent what I call the linear and non-linear domains of human existence. While the linear domain is the planning, there is this whole other non-linear domain I call *intention*.

Planning refers to the left-brain, analytical, sequenced mind, which brings order to our daily lives. Intention refers to the right brain, creative, intuitive capacities that we all possess. In order to calm the chaos you must live at the intersection of your right and left-brain capacities and to move through life with clarity, purpose and power.

The action of planning means that you invest the time and mental energy necessary to organize your life. You bring order to your activities, commitments, belongings, paperwork, goals and future vision. So often our lives spiral into chaos due to lack of planning, simply not stopping long enough to ask some basic questions such as:

- What am I trying to accomplish here?
- What would make the most sense for me to focus on in this day/hour/week?
- What do I want to experience?
- How do I want to feel?
- What will feel good to accomplish today?

Intention means holding a mental image or thought about what you would like to have or experience in your life. An intention is different from a goal in that intention does not have an action plan and timeline associated with it. For example, a *goal* to lose ten pounds would include action steps such as keeping a daily food log, getting 45 minutes of cardiovascular exercise per day and decreasing caloric intake. An *intention* to lose ten pounds might include an image of how your body would look and feel combined with an affirmative statement about your body being fit and healthy.

I had an intention of living in a waterfront home for many years, but did not do anything about that intention until the year 2000. I drew the intention closer to me when I rented an apartment on "Pond Street." I got excited about what I call "approximating my intention"—by living on Pond Street, I was getting closer to having a waterfront home. My next move was to rent a house on a small lake, and from there I finally purchased my lakefront home, and now am blessed to own not one, but two waterfront homes. I did not set out with a specific savings plan, working with a real estate agent or anything of the sort. I held the intention in mind for many years and eventually drew the experience to myself (twice!).

There is tremendous power to that which we consistently hold in mind. There are many quips that point to this such as "What you think about, you bring about." Or "Thoughts held in mind produce after their kind." There is *energy* to our mental and emotional world that we can learn to harness for our highest good. When we think happier thoughts, our energetic vibration literally rises. We become "more attractive" physically and energetically. There is something of a magic, Midas touch that comes with being a "high energy, high vibration" person.

This process of learning to intentionally raise our energy is aided by the function of our left-brain analytical mind through planning our days and our lives. This ongoing activity keeps our desires and goals on our mental radar and on our schedule! The process is further aided by the function of the right brain by channeling our emotional responses in particular ways that create more ease and grace. Calming the chaos in this way trains you to draw from both sides of the brain, "managing your Self in time" rather than managing time. It is truly only in learning to manage yourself that life mastery begins.

Chapter Nineteen

Organize Your Mind

*Set peace of mind as your highest goal and
organize your life around it.*

~Brian Tracy, business leader, speaker, author

In order to begin calming your mind, you have to bring order to your mind. How do you bring order to anything? Well, you organize it, right? So how do you organize your mind? To wrap your head around this idea of organizing your mind, let's bring a parallel to how you organize physical things. If you want to organize your garage, for example, what is a reasonable first step? (No, not calling 1-800-Got-Junk, that comes later!). The first step is to *take everything out of the garage so you can actually begin seeing what is in there.* You cannot organize what you cannot see. Most likely, your mind is a little too much like your cluttered garage (sorry, bad analogy but it works here!). Your mind is too full of things that are probably useful and important, but you cannot really gain access to them because they are cluttered, disorganized and in disarray.

Just like you would need to take everything out of the garage and set it out on the driveway to see what's in there, you have got to get everything out of your mind in order to begin organizing it. How do you do that? How do you get everything out of your mind?

I'm going to give you an exercise that may seem completely off the wall and overwhelming at first, but I have done this with thousands of people and it is amazing to see what happens when you get into it, and how much fun it can actually be. Play along—this is really an essential component to this whole notion of calming the chaos!

Step One: Capture All of It

The exercise is this: Write down everything you have to do, and everything you want to do, have, create, learn, experience and contribute in your life between now and when you die! Yes, that's right, I want you to literally *empty your mind of all the clutter!* You cannot organize your inner world until you begin sorting out what's in there. So the first step to calming the chaos is to write down on a list to capture all of it—all that you want to and have to do between now and when you die.

This list is not to be confused with what some people call your "Bucket List." A Bucket List is only the things you *want to do before you die.* The list I am asking you to create, which I call your Everything List, is what you want to do— your dreams, hopes and aspirations—and what you "have to do," such as going to work, paying the bills, getting a haircut, filing your taxes, exercising, cooking, shopping, reading, updating your Facebook status and the rest of it. Write down EVERTHING you do on one list, in one place. I promise you of all the lists I have ever seen (and I have seen a lot of them), I have never gotten more than four or five pages of written material.

The point of writing down everything you have to do and want to do for the rest of your life is two-fold. On the one hand, it helps you capture the whole of your life (which we often feel is overwhelming) so that you can then go on to step two and three of this system and organize your mind. There is another benefit to this exercise. You may walk around feeling so overwhelmed with all you have to do, that when you actually put it all down on a few pieces of paper and look at it, there is this odd sense of "That's it? That's all I have been so stressed out about? This is it? This is all I am going to be doing with the rest of my life?" It is a sort of strange relief and letdown all at the same time. You may even actually get present to the notion that you need a bigger life!

Now, of course, this list is not exhaustive nor a one-time creation. You will always keep coming up with new, exciting, fun things that you want to have and experience in life and it is very likely that you will also end up having a lot more new things that you "have to do" as well. For example, my son is only nine years old, and one of the things on my list is to help him find the right and perfect college, but when that time actually comes, he may decide to go into the military or start a business or run away with the circus for all I know, so my list will have to change. So the point of the list is not for it to be a one-and-done sort of document. It is an organic document that will become part of your self-management and self-mastery system.

To help you get starting in your thinking, I am including a sample list here for you to look over and get your creative juices flowing.

Do laundry

Food shopping

Cook meals

Plan meals

Clean the house

Pick up after others

Clean out the refrigerator

Clean the cat litter box

Take the cat to the vet

Morning routine

Go to dry cleaners

Go to the tailor

Go to team meetings at work

Staff meetings

Management meetings

Prepare agendas for staff and team meetings

Take and return phone calls

Read and respond to emails

Write performance evaluations

Supervision meetings

Commute to work

Stop for coffee

Lunch meetings

Attend family gatherings

Go to holiday parties

Run, bike and work out

Swim

Play tennis

Ski in the Alps, Utah, Nevada and Colorado

Go to the movies, watch TV

Finalize my estate plan

Leave a million dollars to my kids

Leave money to my church

Get a will done

Decide where to be buried

Go fishing in Alaska

Go to Paris

Run a half marathon

Hike the Grand Canyon

Learn to surf

Learn Spanish

Learn Calligraphy

Take workshops

Attend board meetings

Write board reports

Write social media posts

Research social media material

Update web site

Meet with my boss

Update company training calendar

Plan training sessions

Set up training contracts with subcontractors

Send invoices

Drop off and pick up my child at school

Go to parent meetings

Go to events for my child

Date nights with spouse

Have friends over for dinner

Ski trips

Plan vacations

Go to the beach

Pray

Go to church

Meditate

Read

Journaling

Write goals

Hire a coach

Plan holidays with my family

Go hiking for day trips

Get massages

Take vitamins

Go to the dentist

Get a colonoscopy

Get a mammogram

Get an annual physical

Declutter the garage

Declutter the attic

Declutter the closets

Call repairmen to fix stuff that gets broken

Organize my files at home and work

Throw out old files

Meet with my financial planner about retirement

File things at home and work

Lose 10 pounds

Learn to cook healthy, vegetarian meals

Renovate kitchen

Build a second home

Build an addition to the house

Professionally landscape the yard

Christmas shopping

Fill out financial aid forms

Prepare taxes

File taxes

Choir rehearsals

Go to networking events

Doctor's appointments

Dentist appointments

Physical therapy appointments

Haircut appointments

Pay bills

Go to Bora Bora and Hawaii

Go to Australia

Go to New Zealand

Do a humanitarian mission somewhere

Do spiritual retreats

Go on a bike tour in Europe

Have tea in the garden at the White House

Get car serviced

Take out trash and recycling

Have a NY Times best-selling book

Set up a compost

Find a publisher

Learn video editing

Watch movies/ videos

Tour old churches in Europe

Go to birding in the Amazon

Attend the Olympics

Write a book (or more)

Find an agent

Learn advanced photography

Meet with my coach

Yard work

Learn to play the guitar

Shop for new clothes

Chiropractor appointments

Write blog posts

Read blog posts

Education fund deposits

Go to continuing education programs

Swim with wild dolphins

> *When everything you have to do only lives in your mind, it feels endless.*

You can see from the list above that some of these items are fun and adventurous while others are simple and mundane. You will also notice that the list is not endless. When everything that you have to do only lives in your mind it *feels endless*. Part of the point of this exercise is to contain the chaos, because everything there is for you to do, learn, experience and contribute in life is not endless. While everything that you *could do* in life may be endless, your own unique slice of it, what you actually have interest in or desire, is not.

Go ahead and use this page to start writing your list here.

Write Your "Everything List"

_____   _____

_____   _____

_____   _____

_____   _____

_____   _____

_____   _____

_____   _____

_____   _____

_____   _____

_____   _____

_____   _____

_____   _____

_____   _____

_____   _____

Now that you have taken the time to create your list, keep adding to it over the coming days and weeks. I suggest you actually create a note in your memo pad or notes pages on your smartphone or tablet called your "Everything List" so you can just jot down items as they come to mind. It can be fun and incredibly freeing to get the whole of your life's activities and dreams located in one place!

Step Two: Establishing Your Dreams and Intentions

The next step after capturing all of it is to, of course, *begin organizing it*. Break the list down by placing all of the items you are not currently working on or doing anything about on a separate list. Those items that are simply dreams and you have no intention of doing anything about them right now. You are not planning anything for these, you are not saving money to do them, and you are doing nothing directly to bring these things into your life. They are what I call your intentions or your dreams list. In fact, I call mine my "Sacred Intentions List." I call it my Sacred Intentions because it serves as a constant reminder that my life is a sacred gift and that my dreams and intentions are uniquely mine, directly put into my heart by God, for me to enjoy and pursue. In order to calm the chaos, you have to get in touch with yourself at this deeper level. You have to allow yourself to feel your feelings and explore your passions and desires, rather than put them away as childish notions. I believe that what we most desire, those persistent yearnings of our heart are what make you uniquely "you."

Holding the list in this way gives it a whole different context than simply "What I hope to do before I die." Labeling this list of desired experiences "Sacred Intentions" has a higher consciousness to it, and that is how I want to live my life. Call the list whatever you want, but create a list in your database, and move all of the items that you are *not currently working on* to that list. Using the example above, it would look something like this:

My Sacred Intentions List:

Go to Bora Bora and Hawaii	Ski in the Alps, Utah, Nevada and Colorado
Go to Australia	Finalize my estate plan
Go to New Zealand	Leave a million dollars to my kids
Do a humanitarian	

mission somewhere

Do spiritual retreats

Go on a bike tour in Europe

Tour old churches in Europe

Go to birding in the Amazon

Attend the Olympics

Find an agent

Meet with my coach

Learn to play the guitar

Swim with wild dolphins

Have tea in the garden at the White House

Leave money to my church

Go to fishing in Alaska

Go to Paris

Run a half marathon

Hike the Grand Canyon

Learn to surf

Learn Spanish

Learn Calligraphy

Build a second home

Build an addition to the house

Have a NY Times best-selling book

This list is not my personal Sacred Intentions List, but there are some pretty cool items here. This list is a compilation of the many I have seen over the years mixed in with a few of my own. Feel free to borrow any of these that speak to your heart! But the work here is for you to sit down with *your* Everything List, circle those items that are just dreams, then move them to your database as a list of your hopes and dreams. Why do this? Why create a list of things you hope to do someday or dream of doing? There are many reasons so let's get into that a little bit here.

Creating a list of your dreams and intentions creates what I call an "energetic placeholder" for the things you wish to bring into your life. It is not something that you have to reference all the time, but it is something that you have given your attention and positive emotion to. Remember that I said that creating a positive context is one of the elements of living a high-consciousness life, and that living a high-consciousness life makes you more of a magnet to your good? This list is the central component of that magnetic force. Here's a simple example from my own life.

As my speaking career grew, I wanted to step out and play a bigger game. I felt the desire to do a TED talk as one measure of being recognized as a good speaker and a thought leader. (TED talks are considered to be the epitome of cutting-edge thinking. They are 20-minute talks on any imaginable subject. The TED motto is "Ideas Worth Spreading." Check them out at www.TED.com) I took out my smartphone and added to my Sacred Intentions list, "Do a TED talk" and then simply put it away.

A month or so later I was teaching the use of vision boards to solidify your intentions in one of my programs, so I found some images of TED conferences and added a few of them to my own vision board. Within a couple of months after that, a colleague of mine got a license to do a local TED event and contacted me about her event. I had no idea she was even trying to get a TED license (no easy feat). Her words blew me away. She sent me a message that read, "Jackie, I just got a license from TED and will be producing TEDxWaldenPond in two months. You were the first person I

171

thought of when I got the license. Would you be interested in speaking at my event?"

Would I be interested!?!? I was thrilled and immediately accepted her invitation.

This is an example of the power of the non-linear domain, the field of intention. I merely put the thought out there on my Sacred Intentions List, put a few images on my vision board, and then went about the business of being a speaker (while keeping my energy in high-consciousness). I was in action around what I wanted, in that I was continuing to work as a speaker, booking gigs, doing a good job where I showed up, but I was doing nothing in direct correlation to my TEDx invitation. It was non-linear: X + Y = A rather than Z.

Paying attention to your dreams has another component to it that I believe relates to living a high-consciousness life. When we are living in chronic overwhelm and chaos there is no room to dream, no room to explore your deeper sense of self and what you want from life.

As a coach and spiritual teacher, I give a lot of importance to our dreams. I believe that the desires of your heart are your unique spiritual fingerprint that communicates what you are here to deliver. The dreams I am referring to here are not so much about material possessions for fame, fortune and fast cars (although the fast car part would be OK with me!). I am talking about the deeper longings of our heart for self-expression.

I have reinvented myself time and time again, all in service of seeking to grow and express more of my highest Self. That is what we are here to do. Not to live confined to our fear of change or to the convention of our culture. I left a successful career as an inpatient psychiatric unit director in my early 30s to pursue starting my own business, dove into motherhood in my early 40s and am now reinventing myself as an author and speaker in my 50s. None of these changes came to me lightly; each felt like a direct correspondence from God to keep reaching higher and experience more of life, and most of all, to give more to life.

I wrote earlier that it is easier living in the lower realms of consciousness where you can shirk these kinds of challenges by pointing to all of the external reasons for why you cannot change. That indeed is easier than doing the hard work of facing your fears, learning new skills, taking on new routines and living with an open heart in the face of failure. But it is not nearly as full, rich and expansive as knowing that you can meet any challenge, dream and intention with faith rather than fear and move forward expressing what you feel in your heart is your highest, deepest, truest expression. You would only choose to live this way if you have a passion for something beyond the ordinary—and since you are reading this book I know you are one of those passionate ones!

Let that passion fuel you as we move forward to the next—and most challenging—step of this process.

Step Three: Scheduling Your Self in Time

Your list now should be somewhat shorter and is comprised of the things you are currently doing in your life or planning to do in the near future. This is my favorite part of calming the chaos—it is like when we pull out the whip and chair and fight off the lion in the cage. This next piece has a wonderful surprise element to it that is like a Christmas gift. The gift is that when you finish, *and then live by*, this next piece **you will never have to use a "to do list" again!** Yes, that's right, after you finish and then incorporate this next piece of calming the chaos, you will never again have to live with a to-do list.

Now some of you are perplexed, some of you are relieved and some of you are horrified at the thought of never having a to-do list again. Just notice your reaction to reading that notion and if you are horrified by this thought, you will see where you are attached to doing life the way you have been doing it. But remember, if you keep doing what you have been doing, you will keep getting what you have been getting. Similar actions produce similar results.

By saying you will never have a to-do list again, I do not mean that you will not be capturing and organizing the things you need to do. In fact, you will be doing *so much more* than keeping a to-do list, because it is crucial that you get things out of your head and into a system that keeps your mind organized and that is oriented *in time*.

What system am I talking about? Your schedule! I feel like I can hear a collective groan across the nation. Yes, your schedule! Your schedule is a *time-bound structure* to keep your mind organized and keep you moving toward the things you desire. I teach such a radically different way of scheduling; it is all about this notion of creating your life in alignment with your values, based on what you love, in the highest consciousness, keeping your mind clear to stay in action on what is important to you. How I teach scheduling brings the two domains of content and context, linear and non-linear together.

Another major cause of stress is saying you will do more in a given hour or day or week than you are capable of accomplishing. This occurs over and over again because for the most part, you have no relationship to time!

What you will begin learning as you schedule yourself in time is how long things actually take. When you live your life with no relationship to time you truly have no clue how long things take! Every time I say this in a seminar I get a room full of head-nods asserting the truth of this statement. We repeatedly grossly underestimate how long most things take to complete or accomplish. Learning to schedule yourself in time helps you become more productive and less stressed, but not until you deal with the degree you have been living in some delusion about your ability to get far more done in a given timeframe than is reasonable.

I often say that we are "psychotic" with regard to our relationship with time! Yes, I am a trained mental health professional so I can say things like that! Psychosis means that a person has experienced a "break with reality" in terms of how things are perceived. When it comes to time, what I observe over and over again is that most people have no bearing with reality! We are a culture that is psychotic with regard to time!

Once you start managing yourself in relation to time, actually scheduling what you are doing and when you are doing it, you will begin to establish a relationship with time *in reality* rather than in an illusion. Learning how long things actually take leads you to make better decisions regarding what you commit to doing with your time. While putting things on your schedule, you can start recognizing and saying to yourself, *"That's crazy. Who designed that? I don't want that life"* and then you are able to make choices that are more in line with the life that you actually want to be living, not the one that has been living you.

So let me ask you, "What do you put on your schedule?" Appointments with people, meetings, phone calls, errands? Is the majority of what goes on your schedule the things you "have to do" for work or for someone else? Most often what people put on their schedules are just the face-to-face appointments where you physically have to be somewhere to do something with or for someone else.

What about the rest of what you have to and want to do in life? What about commuting to work, preparing for meetings, writing reports or any of the collateral tasks associated with your job or with raising your children? Where do those things live? And what about those activities you long to do but never honor the time to do them? Things like reading, rejuvenation, connecting with your spouse, meditation or other spiritual practice or simply downtime. Where do these nurturing activities live? Where are they represented? They are not. They stay in your head, and as we already saw, your head can only capture so much data before going into overload. That is why everyone is walking around in chaos and frenzy, with overloaded circuitry, feeling stressed out and depleted. You are likely carrying more in your head than you have the neurological capacity to hold and process, therefore feeling on chronic overload.

It is what Edward Hallowell, the founder of the adult Attention Deficit Disorder movement, calls "attention deficit traits," which he claims are epidemic in organizations. The answer is to get the overload of data out of your head and into your schedule. All that is required is that you train yourself in how to bring the high-consciousness principle of order to the planning of your days and your life.

Far too often to-do lists are a setup for failure because they have *no bearing in time.* When you have a long list of things you want to accomplish and yet no correlation to how long those things take, you are bound to not get through them by the end of the day, or week, or month. Then you walk around with this incredibly disempowering inner conversation of "What is wrong with me? Why can't I get it all done? I need to be more productive." Or an outer directed conversation of, "What is wrong with them (boss, managers, spouses)? Can't they see that I am running on all cylinders here? They are trying to run me into the ground. They have no idea how hard I am working, and the bottom line is they don't care." Looking at these two sets of conversations, what level of consciousness does this reflect? Obviously these are low-energy conversations.

Similarly, the commonly taught A,B,C prioritization method is an equal setup for failure because it too has *no bearing in time.* I've worked with many coaching clients over the years who were trained in this method before coming to me for coaching, and none of them got to their "C" items, which resulted in the same self-defeating conversations and less than optimal productivity.

So what do you do instead? How do you move through life with planning and order in a way that supports what you are doing and how you are feeling? One huge paradigm shift begins by creating a new context for the way that you hold and relate to your schedule. Do you remember how I define context? A context is the energetic or attitudinal environment inside of which something lives. The context of something gives rise to our experience of that thing. So how do you relate to and feel about your schedule? If you feel like it is a "ball and chain" tying you down to an endless and meaningless list of things you "have to get done," you can clearly see that this is not a context that will inspire you, lift you up and expand your energy.

> *Your schedule can be a meaningful, fluid, organic structure that provides the container and accountability for you to live an empowered, balanced and joyful life.*

Consider that your schedule can begin living for you, not as just a list of things you have to do, but as a meaningful, organic, fluid structure that provides the container and accountability for you to live an empowered, balanced and joyful life. Somehow I will bet that is a new paradigm for you! Imagine that you can relate to your schedule like it is the container inside of which your life is reflected back to you; a contract of sorts between your day-to-day self and your "higher Self." By higher Self, I mean the part of you that is connected to God or Spirit or whatever notion you choose to represent the Wholeness of Life. Wrap your head around that for a minute! A contract between you and God! How does that feel vis-à-vis your former notion that your schedule is simply a place to write down the things you had to get done?

A contract is an agreement or a commitment in writing with regard to what you agree to do. Contracts provide clarity and accountability. They define the parameters of something. A contract is a *binding agreement*. When you enter into a contract with someone, you are giving your word. Do you relate to your schedule in this way?

Most often, we relate to agreements we make to other people in a higher fashion than agreements we make with ourselves. Can you see that you relate in a more serious, thoughtful way with what you do for another person than you do for yourself? Doing this to an excessive degree (which many of us do) eventually leads to depleting rather than restoring your energy. Similarly, *only* doing for self and not for others can have a similar depleting effect. It is in plugging into that endless cycle of giving and receiving that we are made whole.

This notion of a contract binds these two elements together: the greater *context* that contains the *content* of your life. You represent the whole of yourself on your schedule through paying attention to

> *You have to practice scheduling yourself in time.*

how you feel and then planning your schedule with intention.

Your schedule should be a binding agreement between your content and your context. It should represent both what you are doing and what you value. You have to practice scheduling your whole Self in time because that is really what you are here for: the greater context of your life and who you are.

You also want the relief of being present in the moment, of actually feeling off when you're off, or enjoying your kids when you are with them, and being able to focus on one thing at a time. So often you are mentally at work when you are having dinner with the kids, or texting friends when you are at work. There is such a loss of connection to both our inner world and our relationships when we are mentally in a hundred different places at any one time. It becomes addictive to be constantly distracted and stimulated. If you don't have enough outer distractions, you find inner distractions to replace them. You can get so caught up in the adrenal overload that you find yourself wildly uncomfortable with the notion of slowing down or even—heaven forbid—stopping for a time.

Learning to plan your life and live your plan quiets this inner turmoil. So what do you put on your schedule? Well, I suppose the answer to that is *everything* that you are doing. You will only begin calming the chaos when you start getting present to what you are doing and when you are doing it. You have got to get clear on how many things you are saying "yes" to in any given day or week in order to stay even remotely out of overwhelm. Remember, if you are a "yes" to everything, you will be a "no" to your peace of mind. The only way you can really know how much you are doing is to be able to see it all in front of you, in a concrete structure that shows you when you are already committed and when you are free.

Does this mean you have to put brushing your teeth on your schedule? No, that's silly! However, you do want to put something that represents your morning routine on your schedule! Remember my coaching client who was about to get fired from his job because he believed it took him a half hour to do his morning routine, and then he learned it took him 45 minutes? You may well be that person. So you put things on your schedule that you are doing, and when you are doing them. Of course you will have to move some items from time to time, because unexpected events occur. But you at least have your schedule to guide you through the day and help you know what you are going to accomplish and enjoy each day.

You often walk through your day feeling overwhelmed and knowing you have so much to do, but what happens when you actually have a couple of hours with no meetings or no place you have to go? Do you sit down and become wildly productive ticking things off that you know you want to accomplish? No, you don't, do you? Do you know what happens when you have that open space in your schedule and there is so much in your head? Your mind goes into a blur or what I call "the dumb air" and you can't think straight. So you do busy work; a little bit of this, a little bit of that, a few emails, check your Facebook page, read the news online, go chat with your office mate about the meeting everyone was upset about last week, and then at the end of all of that busy work you only have a half hour left before your next meeting so you can't start anything too involved in such a short period of time! That is exactly what it looks like for so many people. And it is not your fault. It is not because you are lazy, disorganized or inefficient; *you are simply not trained in managing your Self in time.*

Rather than this, here is how you can begin to schedule yourself in time:

First, you will need to spend a couple of hours getting all of your daily activities set up on your calendar. I know that you don't know when you are going to do each event, but here's the trick–*MAKE IT UP!* Having a template to guide you will make you so much more effective than doing what you have been doing. And as you practice scheduling yourself in time, you will actually get better at it and it will come more naturally to you. Just like any new skill, you have to start small, practice a lot, make mistakes and learn as you go; but if you stay with it, I promise you it will result in you finally calming the chaos and knowing true peace of mind.

Begin by locating as many of the things from your Everything List into your schedule in a particular time slot on a given day. For example, every quarter I schedule "review quarterly goals" for the first Monday of the quarter at 9 a.m. If I am asked to speak at a conference or run a training program on that particular Monday, I just move the appointment with myself. Do you see how it functions as a placeholder for what you want to be doing instead of holding it in your head? When I schedule the other event, I simply move the appointment to review my goals to another time. It will require some mental effort to move these items into your schedule, but you can do it. Invest in yourself in a new way.

You will have to schedule things out further in time to accommodate all of the items that you have been keeping in your head. Most people just schedule things a day to a week in advance, but using this method, you will likely start scheduling things several weeks or even months into the future. And be sure to schedule the things you *want to do not just the things you feel you have to do!*

That does not mean there isn't room for spontaneity! Remember, this is *YOUR* schedule and you can do whatever you want with it. Daily listen within. Follow your heart and your intuition. Suppose you have scheduled on a given Saturday to clean the attic or garage, and then the day before you are all set to begin this project, you get a call from a high school friend who is in town for the weekend and she can only get together with you on Saturday. Do you rigidly say, "Oh, I'm sorry, I am scheduled to clean out my garage"? Of course not! (Well, only if you don't want to hang out with her!) You simply go to your schedule and adjust accordingly. You either get up an hour earlier and still do a few hours of garage cleaning, then go out with your friend, or you reschedule the task altogether. The point is not to have you rigidly locked into anything—it is to give you structure, clarity and peace of mind.

This system does not limit your freedom. It *creates freedom!* That may sound counterintuitive as you think about bringing this level of order and organization to the living of your life, but here is something to ponder; there is no freedom without the freedom to express your deepest, most true Self. By "Self" I am referring to your highest expression, your true purpose, your most divine nature. There is not freedom in life when you are living in chaos, uncertain about what your life is for or how to move toward what your heart is calling you to pursue. This system addresses that challenge head on. It provides you with tools and structures to bring forth your deepest desires and passions, as well as increasing what you deliver to this world. I don't know what is more exciting and freeing than that!

Chapter Twenty

Self-Management Practices

Time management is really a misnomer. The challenge is not to manage time but to manage ourselves. The key is not to prioritize what's on your schedule, but to schedule your priorities.

~Steven Covey, business leader, author

Once you have established your schedule based on your Everything List, there are certain practices that will support you in living inside of this system and will keep your mind free and clear. Here are a few things to put in place:

Use the recurring events function on your electronic calendar for as many items as you can, so you only have to enter them once. For example, I have my daily morning routine, driving my son to and from school, and the once-per-week "take out the trash" items on my calendar as recurring events so I only had to enter them once even though they recur multiple times.

Touch base with your schedule every day at the beginning and end of your day. Start each day just going over what is on your schedule. Allow yourself set the tone for the energy of your day, and remember to set it in high consciousness. Look at where you need to be and what you need for each appointment, and be sure you have the necessary items for the meetings or appointments you have. Then at the end of the day, go over your day and see what things you did not accomplish that were on your schedule and (this is critical) *move those items to another time slot in your schedule!* Do not keep them in your head! End your day appreciating all that you accomplished (high consciousness) rather than beating yourself up for what you didn't do or blaming others for getting in your way (low consciousness).

The last practice that keeps this system strong and keeps the chaos at bay is what I call the Three Strikes Rule. The Three Strikes Rule means that you only get to move an item on your schedule three times before you have to really look and see if you are simply avoiding it rather than needing to reschedule it.

> *Procrastination is a huge energy drain!*

When you move an item repeatedly, it is simply another form of procrastination, and procrastination is a huge energy drain! Avoiding doing things that you don't want to do or are too challenged by is an energy drain. Too often we don't tackle the hard mental work of our jobs; we stay busy doing email and other forms of busywork. This is just a mental habit and you can retrain yourself to move from being busy to being productive. It requires managing yourself in a new and different way; and the Three Strikes Rule is one access to doing that because this rule forces you to tell the truth about the items you are moving. Are you committed to the item or not? Do you have the skills for it or not? Do you need some accountability around it? It is not that you "didn't have time." You are moving things because you are not choosing to fulfill them when you said you would and there is an enormous cost to doing that repeatedly— It costs you vitality, enthusiasm, accomplishment and peace of mind.

I worked with a coaching client using this self-management system, and he was actually sending me his schedule weekly so he could truly practice and be held accountable for what he was doing and how he was managing himself in time. I noticed one item seemed to show up many times. So, I asked him what was happening that this item kept getting moved, and I noted that it seemed to have been moved more than three times. The item was writing a scholarly article for a professional publication.

He admitted that in fact he had moved it six times.

I said, "So what's the deal? Are you going to do it? If not, move the item to your Intentions List so it does not become an energy drain for you. It's okay. There's still a place to keep it in a structure so you don't forget that you want to do it. You will see it there when you review your intentions."

He said, "No, no, no — I'm going to do it."

I said, "OK, before our call next week, do what you need to do to get that article hammered out." I gave him accountability and support, and with that he completed the article and submitted it the next month. It turned out that he actually won a national award on the piece he submitted. That was not going to happen if he didn't manage himself in time.

I am certain you can think of accomplishments you have wanted to pursue but you just haven't managed yourself. Do you see how it costs you? It costs you self-esteem and accomplishment, but it also costs the world your full contribution in life. This is why this program is so vitally important; it gets you fully engaged in what is important to you and has you deliver at a much higher level in life.

As you manage *yourself* rather than your *time and stress*, you will notice more about your work habits such as lack of planning, procrastination, doing busywork rather than the longer, more difficult mental work, overscheduling yourself so that you cannot complete things fully. These are the work habits that drain your energy and keep you in chaos.

The fundamental reason to learn to manage your energy rather than your time is simply this: you will feel better. You will come to *trust yourself* in a new way and you will like the person you become as a result. Calming the chaos begins and ends with you. Our culture is not going to slow down, technology is not going to come up with some radical breakthrough to make you feel better. Things do not change, people do. Living in higher consciousness has you focus more on your inner world and responses, which leads to the desire to develop new skills. It is time for you to make this change. You can do it. In fact your life may very well depend on it!

Chapter Twenty-One

Complete Your Day

*Always aim at complete harmony of thought and word
and deed. Always aim at purifying your thoughts and
everything will be well.*

~Mahatma Gandhi, spiritual and political leader

There is one more structure that is integral to calming the chaos and the whole system I teach for managing yourself in time. It is a practice called your "Daily Debrief." This practice should be employed at the end of your workday or the end of your day at home, whichever you prefer. Your Daily Debrief allows you to reflect, reschedule and schedule any new activities and tasks that arose you moved through your day.

Dealing with Incomplete Tasks

In your Daily Debrief, you open your schedule and look to see, "What did I accomplish today? How did I feel? Did I do everything that I said I was going to do? Is my schedule complete?" If not, simply relocate any incomplete items to a different time and day. If you didn't fulfill a commitment ,or if a task took longer than you expected, move it forward in your schedule. Whatever you did not complete, simply reschedule it. The goal here is to not keep your commitments and activities in your head, but to locate everything on your schedule. With this system of managing yourself rather than time, you are actually moving projects from implementation to completion.

> *If things took much longer than you expected, just move them forward in your schedule.*

When you don't reschedule incomplete tasks, they live in your mind, and your mind gets cluttered. The new practice is to look at your schedule and say, "I didn't finish this project today by three, but Friday morning I've got an opening, and I can get that completed then." This is how to stay *productive, not busy.*

The Mental Energy of Learning New Tricks

By the way, don't be surprised if the mental work of thinking through your activities in time exhausts you, if you're not already a little exhausted just thinking about it. It is important for you to understand that you will feel fatigued and even a little bit irritable as you begin using this method of managing yourself rather than time. The reason for that is neurological. The brain is not the most sophisticated organ. It likes to operate by, "Let's just do the same thing over and over and over again. Then I don't have to expend much energy. I can just keep humming along." The brain creates these little things called *neural pathways* that help you operate by rote without requiring much thinking, thereby not requiring much energy. You know very well that you can drive from your house to your office or to the grocery store without having to think about it. You can cook an entire meal without much thought if you have done it often enough. That is the result of neurological programming. Neuropathways are little "ruts" in your brain that are created with repetition. They are useful except when we form habits that don't support the most effective way of living.

In order to "unlearn" and re-learn new patterns of behavior, such as I am suggesting here, you have to create new neuropathways — and that will make you tired for a short while and perhaps even a little irritable. But it is worth it! If you stick with learning to schedule yourself in a new way, the tremendous benefits will amaze you. You will become the least stressed, most productive person you know!

In line with that, you might want to schedule yourself a little more lightly as you begin learning this process, because it will require more mental energy to learn how to think and operate in this way. The reason that young children need a lot more sleep than adults do is because they are constantly learning, and their brains need to be recharged. So please be mindful to get a little more sleep as you begin training yourself in these new skills. Schedule yourself more lightly and go deeply into this work.

In order to learn how long your various activities actually take, begin by estimating how long you think a task will take, *and then double it*, and you'll be somewhere in the ballpark of how long it actually takes. If you find yourself having extra time, do whatever you want! You can move on to the next thing or surf the net, you can go out to lunch, take a nap, or do whatever you want. Scheduling yourself in time increases your productivity, which ultimately increases your freedom.

Scheduling What You Want to Experience and Create

Here is another suggestion that is a small but profound shift. Too often our schedules feel like just a long "to do" list, rather than a placeholder for the inspiring, committed and high consciousness life we want to lead. To counter that, you can begin writing in your schedule what you want to experience or create rather than what you "have to do." In my evening time, when I know I am going to be with my son, rather than just putting "Nathan care" in my schedule, I write "Enjoy spending the evening with Nathan" or "Pay attention to Nathan as he grows into a fine young man." Do you see the difference? Rather than "workout" for your fitness time, you can write, "Creating maximum health and wellness in my body." I am suggesting you literally *put these phrases in your schedule* to reflect that your life is more than a series of "to do's" but shift to begin creating the experiences you want to have.

Chapter Twenty-Two

Dealing with Life More Effectively

Being organized isn't about giving away everything you own or trying to become a different person; it's about living the way you want to live, but better.

~Andrew Mellen, author, professional organizer

Let's look at some of the skills that will have you living more efficiently and effectively. These are further teachings in managing yourself rather than time and stress! Make a goal of adding *one new skill each month* for the next several months, then just really stick with it.

Mail, Bills, Paperwork

Mail: Go through your mail as soon as you receive it and immediately put anything away that you don't want into the recycling bin.

Catalogs: These create a lot of paper clutter in the home. Don't let it happen! Follow this rule: If you get a bunch of catalogs and they look nice, but you're not going to order from them that week, they

> *Go through your mail as soon as you receive it.*

go into the recycling bin. If you decide you need something in one of them, you can always find it online!

Magazines: It is helpful to practice that as a new issue comes in, the old issue goes out. Anything else is going to clutter up your space and your mind.

Bills: There are two alternative ways to handle bills. Either they come in and you pay them, and then you throw away what's unnecessary and file everything you need to keep for your records, and it's done. The other alternative for paying bills is to have a bill slot or drawer in your desk at your home office where you put your bills, and schedule appointment with yourself once a week to pay them.

Filing and Paperwork: File any needed papers immediately upon receiving them. Or if there is an action that needs to be taken on a piece of paperwork, there are two possible ways of handling it. Either take the required action right then, using the "do-it-right-now" approach, or enter on your schedule a time to do it. Each piece of paper should be handled minimally. For example, you get applications or forms from the insurance company, and you need to get back to them. If you cannot do it right then, put it in your bill drawer and deal with it when you have your once-a-week appointment with yourself. Don't leave it out on the counter or your desk to clutter your space and your mind.

Clothes, Dishes and Laundry: The general rule with household things is "touch it only once." This means that when you take something out, you use it and then you place it back where it belongs. Developing this habit

> *Touch it only once.*

194

significantly reduces the amount of time that you spend tidying up as well as looking for things that you have misplaced. "Touch it only once" is a great motto. For example, I put my clothes out at night, and then when I come home, they either go back in the drawer or into the laundry. Remember, "Touch it only once!"

Do you know how much time you spend tidying up? One of my motivations for creating this program was how frustrated I became when I would lose weekend after weekend just "keeping up with life's messes." I learned that if I just managed myself differently, I would not have to spend time on it at all. Going through huge stacks of mail, sorting piles of unkempt clothes that have been thrown in the chair, cleaning up dirty dishes and picking up the house would eat up my entire weekend. But I learned that it doesn't have to be that way. By managing myself differently and practicing the "touch it only once" rule, I gained a tremendous amount of freedom on my weekends and in my mind!

What is your commitment for your home environment? Personally, I don't want to have a disorganized, messy home where I would run and hide if somebody rang the doorbell. It *feels better* to have a beautiful, harmonious, welcoming environment. Remember, order is a very high-consciousness principle. You can create the environment you want by developing different habits.

Managing Your Goals

Let's talk a little bit about how to manage your goals. Scheduling an annual goal-planning session is a great approach. I do this at the beginning of every year, but you can do it at any time of the year. Sit down and ask yourself what you want to be focused on in this period of your life. What do you want to be using your energy for? What do you want to accomplish?

> *The pursuit of meaningful goals.*

Harvard University professor Dr. Tal Ben-Shahar reports in his book "Happier: Learn the Secrets to Daily Joy and Lasting Fulfillment" (2007) that the mere act of setting and working toward meaningful goals increases your sense of happiness and well-being. Reaching the goal is secondary. It is the pursuit of meaningful goals that engenders greater engagement in life. Reaching the goal is truly not even essential in increasing happiness. It is the process of setting and moving toward things that are meaningful to you that increases happiness.

After determining some meaningful goals, the next step is to break them down into action steps. Action steps tell you specifically what you need to do to move you toward the goals. I believe that the *energy* you create with your intention and action begins a process that hastens your goals toward you.

Then, what do you do with those action steps? Put them in your schedule. Break the goals down into scheduled action steps so you will have a road map leading you to your goal. Remember, whether or not you actually accomplish the goal is not the point. Focusing your life toward what is meaningful to you is the key. Goals help you be productive rather than busy, and fundamentally that just feels better!

People say, "Well, I don't know when I'm going to want to do these action steps." It doesn't matter. The point is to get these activities in your schedule, and then you see that what you desire is actually possible, even if you are taking small steps. You are managing yourself in relation to your goals, not managing your time. Remember to put your activities in language that inspires you too! So rather than "work on my book" you might want to write, "Enjoyed completing section one of my new bestseller!" That will likely call you to action in a new and higher way!

You may also want to schedule a quarterly review of your goals as a way to keep them in existence. Otherwise, there is always the chance that you will move on to the next thing that comes at you—and before you know it you have lost sight of the goals, which gets you right back into the rat race again. The goals can be simple things such as a date night with your spouse or a weekend getaway with some old friends, but getting the things you long to do in your schedule will feed your mind and spirit.

Meditation Skills and Practices

Meditation skills and practices help you to manage your personal energy, your thoughts and your entire inner landscape. You have probably heard this million times, but I will make it the one million and first — *develop a meditation practice.* The benefits of meditation are so significant that if there were a way to take all the benefits and put it into a pill, it would sell like wildfire!

One very common thing I hear from people is, "I tried meditation, but I can't do it." Of course you can't. That's the whole point. Your head will not be quiet the first or second or tenth time you sit to still your mind. The point of meditation, initially, is not to quiet your mind, although people think that that's the whole point.

> *The point is to be able to follow those thoughts, or watch them with an observer's detachment.*

They think, "I'm just going to sit and not have any thoughts." No, you're not. You are going to have thoughts. The point is to be able to follow those thoughts, or watch them with an observer's detachment. You should not get attached to any thoughts. When you notice that you've gone down some tunnel, and you forgotten that you're sitting in meditation, the point is to consciously bring yourself back to your inner awareness, to your breath. Let the thoughts go and return to inner stillness.

I teach a program called "Life Mastery" where I begin teaching meditation by telling participants to simply sit still for three minutes. Don't worry about your mind at all. Just sit still. Learn to quiet your body for three minutes a day. Just as people can master their bodies, they can begin mastering the mind. With enough practice, you can begin sitting quietly for three to five minutes. You will begin to feel the benefit of slowing down. After learning to quiet the body, add a couple of minutes of just counting your breath — simply counting in breath and out breath. That's it. What you will find after just a few seconds is that your mind is no longer focused on the breath. It has gone off thinking of all the things you need to do or what your co-worker said that upset you or the party you are going to tomorrow night. Your mind is almost never still. Training your mind to come to stillness is an amazing approach to managing your energy. It will increase your happiness and ease your anxiety in a way that few other activities ever will. There is no better way to calm the chaos than having a regular meditation practice, even if it's only five minutes a day.

Avoiding Low-Consciousness Media

Be mindful of the types of energy that you expose yourself to through media. As you focus more on managing your energy, it is best to avoid media with violent themes or with themes that are clearly low-consciousness in nature.

A good deal of what is available in mainstream culture will not enhance your energetic consciousness. The places we go, the things we read, watch on TV, listen to and even eat, all impact our overall energy level. Reading or viewing stories about rape, murder and hate crimes serve no purpose when you are committed to living a high-consciousness life. Spending time engaged in addictive behavior, or with people who are chronically negative and blaming, will not enhance your quality of life.

Numerous social science research studies indicate that being exposed to violence, violent themes or hate-laden messages correlates with higher degrees of depression, aggression, anxiety and a decrease in overall compassion and empathy across demographic lines (Anderson, Gentile and Buckley, 2007, Bushman and Anderson, 2009, Hawkins, 2006).

Consuming food that is processed, laden with toxic chemicals or created with inhumane methods creates similar disharmony in your body (Robbins, 2011). The movement toward ethical treatment of animals, environmental sustainability, global resource equity and organic produce is reflective of a small, but growing, subculture of "cultural creatives" (Ray and Anderson, 2001) who subscribe to higher consciousness values. Does your eating reflect your highest sense of yourself? Is it in alignment with your values for wellness, sustainability and nutrition? Or do you eat with no thought to what you are consuming, where it comes from, how your dollars and your choices impact the whole? All of this is reflective of your level of consciousness and energy, and the more you grow in consciousness, the more you will be mindful of what and how you eat. This mindfulness leads to an overall increase in your well-being and state of mind, which in turn serves to raise your consciousness further (Freston, 2006).

Choosing media that reflect high-consciousness values will serve your growth and overall sense of well-being. There are many positive, uplifting, high-energy web-based radio stations such as UnityFM, Wisdom Radio Network and Achieve Radio. There are wonderful movies produced and distributed by Spiritual Cinema Circle. Upbeat magazines such as *Ode*, *Unity*, *Spirituality and Health*, *Science of Mind*,

Shambhala Sun and many more can satisfy our craving for information, while supporting our growth and development.

Chapter Twenty-Three

Top Ten Rules of Calming the Chaos

*The whole point of being alive is to evolve into the
complete person you were intended to be.*

~Oprah Winfrey, actress, talk show host,
cultural icon, businesswoman

I truly believe that the principles in this book will lead
you to "evolve into the complete person you were intended
to be" as Oprah is quoted above. I want to do everything I can
to ensure that you get how simple (but not easy!) these
principles are, so I am doing a Top Ten Rules summary here.
Everyone loves a "Cliff Notes" shortcut to new learning, and
this book wouldn't be complete without one! Below I have
listed out the ten essential components that will help you
calm the chaos by managing your energy rather than your
time and stress.

**1. Become Aware of and Incredibly Willing to Reduce Energy
Drains**

You have got to be willing to do things differently if you
want to experience greater productivity and less stress. One
of the best ways of doing this is by reducing what drains your
energy and increasing what feeds your energy. Say "no" more

often. Align your choices with your values. Be rigorous with scheduling what feeds your soul!

2. Make a Contract with Yourself

Remember that your schedule represents a "contract" between yourself and your higher Self or God. Your schedule represents what you are doing with your life and as such can be related to in a mindful, almost sacred manner. Have your schedule be such a mirrored reflection of who you are that if you die today, anyone could pick up your schedule and live your life. See your schedule as one component of a system that reflects your commitments, values, promises and intentions for now and the rest of your life.

3. Align Your Actions with Your Desires

The key to what others call time management is what I call "self-management"–which means managing your tendency to procrastinate, engage in distractions, or allow busywork to take over your day. You will move from being busy to being productive when you practice solid self-management by aligning your daily actions with your values and desires.

4. Tear Up Your Lists

Remember to locate everything that you can on your schedule, not in your head or on a sticky note or on a to-do list somewhere. The only list-like documents you will keep are your Sacred Intentions. The only exception to this is a list that you make prior to going shopping, which you complete when you are finished. (There are even some good grocery shopping apps that can make it even easier!)

5. Mentally Prepare for Your Day Early

Begin your day by reviewing your schedule to mentally prepare for what you need to deliver, how you feel *and what you want to experience and create*. Be sure you have the materials and resources you need for all of your appointments, commitments, and tasks before leaving home. For example, be sure you have your gym bag if you are going to the gym, an external drive if you need to work on a different computer, or all the materials or books you may need if you are going to work on preparing a meeting or a talk. Schedule times to make calls and, if you don't know the phone number of a person or place you are calling, look it up as you schedule the call and place the phone number in the appointment slot so that you will have it right there when it is time to call. Then, add the number to your database so you won't have to search for it the next time. This applies to restaurants you call, professional services you access, stores you utilize, neighbors and acquaintances.

6. Finish the Day with a Debrief

At the end of every day, go over what you had scheduled and review what you accomplished and what you did not. If there is anything you did not complete, recommit to the action and move that task forward to a new time slot. If new commitments or accountabilities arose during the day, be sure that they also get located into a committed time slot on a different day before you close your day.

7. Complete the Week with a Debrief

Similarly, end your week with a half-hour appointment to debrief your week. Review your week to be sure you have fulfilled all of your commitments or rescheduled them into new time slots. You will also want to look ahead and begin scheduling your next week—and even more—accordingly. For example, if you are doing something in two or three weeks, such as running a big meeting, starting a promotional campaign for your business, or teaching a workshop, you can begin preparing for that deliverable ahead of time by scheduling preparation time for the task. This eliminates a feeling of last-minute overwhelm and improves the quality of your work.

8. Review Your Goals and Intentions Quarterly

Schedule a quarterly review of your goals and intentions so that you have the opportunity to review them and see if they are actions you still want to undertake. This single practice will serve to keep you on track and focused. If you are still committed to a particular goal, and ready to take action, you can start scheduling the action items. Doing a review more often is more powerful, but at least quarterly is needed to maintain a solid and positive relationship with your goals.

9. Use Repeating Events Once

Schedule recurring events once, using the "recurring events" feature on an electronic calendar to have the item repeat weekly, monthly, yearly, or some other repeatable time frame. For example, your daily exercise or spiritual practice can be listed once for the rest of your life!! Just set it for the day and time you have made a commitment to, click "no end date" and it will show up time and time again. You can do this for car inspections, annual checkups, hair appointments, or any recurring meetings, appointments or activities in which you engage.

10. Either Do It, Move It, or Eliminate It

There is a hard and fast rule about moving appointments in your schedule. You get to move an appointment three times and that's it–after that, the item goes off your schedule. After moving it three times, you either have to do it or be honest with yourself that you are not really committed to it. ***Avoiding completing tasks is an enormous energy drain.*** Resisting any activity or circumstance creates negative energy and drains positive energy in and around you. It will only serve to pull you down. If you are still committed to a task, yet struggling, you might want to see some sort of support in accomplishing the action you want to take. The negative energy of procrastination keeps you from feeling a clear, balanced state of mind. It is harder to focus when you are resisting something. Your thoughts and emotions get so clouded with negativity and "I don't want to" energy that you can barely get moving. Inertia is a near constant companion. To counter this, simply accept doing the thing you are resisting. Accept that you have *chosen* this activity (and you have, by the way, even if you are "choosing" it to avoid some negative consequence of not doing it) and mentally surrender your resistance, turning your "have to" into "choose to." You will physically feel a shift when you practice this approach. There is power and magic to the practice of acceptance and surrender.

Use these Ten Rules daily, infuse your life with them, teach them to others and watch your life transform right in front of your eyes. You will truly become one of the least stressed, most productive people you know!

Chapter Twenty-Four

The Path Toward Calm

Never be in a hurry; do everything quietly and in a calm spirit. Do not lose your inner peace for anything whatsoever, even if your whole world seems upset.

~Saint Francis de Sales, honored saint of the Catholic Church

By now you clearly see that this book is not a time management course. It is not a program for managing your to-do list or getting more done in less time. Managing time is easier than managing yourself, because then you can complain about it like it is something outside of you! This approach is about learning to manage your Self *in* time. The whole paradigm shift that this book uncovers is *"Are you going to do what you know is yours to do and will you be who you came here to be?"*

This approach can seem fairly confronting because *it is all about you.* Calming the chaos is about learning to manage yourself based on your consciousness, values, commitments and what you want to produce and experience in life.

> *Are you going to do what you know there is to do?*

There are certain ways that you can design and create your life that will support you in being happier, more effective human being. There are ways of being, skills and practices that you can develop that will absolutely undoubtedly reduce your stress.

The hard truth about our current culture is that too many people are committed to mere survival: They are just getting through one day and getting into the next so they can get it all done. You have probably lived like that to some degree as well.

To live beyond survival, you are learning about managing energy by understanding your level of consciousness. You have come to understand what is draining you and feeding you. Hopefully, some of the activities that feed you made it onto your calendar — spending time with family, taking the kids out, going for a hike, reading for a leisurely afternoon. You are beginning to create rhythms that feed your body, mind and soul. This is the key to living an inspired life: that when you feel inspired and enthused, you are living a spiritual life. Inspiration means "spirit within" and enthusiasm means "God within." That is what I am hoping for– as a result of reading this book and implementing the concepts and strategies herein, you will begin truly living a life that inspires you and that you feel wildly enthused by.

The major theme of this book is learning to master the two planes of existence: the physical and the ethereal–or the seen and unseen planes. It is about mastering the *content* of your life (work, commitments, papers, stuff, relationships) as well as the *context* (attitudes, emotions, beliefs and your overall level of consciousness). As you learn to control your internal states, your outward behavior follows suit.

There is a tremendous amount of material for you to integrate and apply from this book. It is part practical and part philosophical. If you have made it this far you now have a new awareness and understanding of your relationship with time, a new appreciation of what is important to you, a clearer sense of where you have been caught up in the cycle of busyness, rather than being fully productive. You have a new understanding about how to manage your energy; what feeds you and what drains you. Rather than trying to manage time as an enemy, you now see time for the unlimited possibility that it is. You also recognize the degree you have been living with self-defeating and disempowering habits. You now have the tools and awareness to carve out a wholly different experience in life; one in which you are empowered to create what you want, rather than moving unconsciously in the world around you.

How do you make these changes and make them stick? The truth is that behavior change requires two very important components: accountability and practice. I suggested at the very beginning of this book that you get a partner or small group with whom to do this work. If you did not do so at the beginning, you can clearly see by now what benefit that will bring. Doing this work with a group offers support and accountability to make the changes happen and it will encourage you to keep the practice of managing your energy, not your time, in the forefront of your mind. You have got to *practice* because this is not how our culture thinks!

Go back to Section One where you wrote down your intention for change. See if you have already met part or all of that intention. If you have not fulfilled all of it, do you see clearly that you now have the knowledge and tools to do so? I believe you will see that you do, and I believe you can create the changes that you desire.

You are on the way to a new life... and yet the journey has also just begun. The road to this new life can only be traveled with tremendous fortitude. It takes clarity of vision and purpose to learn to say "no" to the unending string of opportunities that will no doubt come your way.

To calm the chaos you must recognize that too much of anything (no matter how cool or great it may seem) is no longer a good thing. You are learning to live your life at a savoring pace, and bringing a deeper sense of meaning and fulfillment into this notion of being human.

The most important thing for you to know, beyond the shadow of a doubt, is that the calm you are seeking is also seeking you. Living in a higher level of consciousness will not solve all of your problems, but imagine what a difference it will make to address practical, day-to-day challenges with this knowledge and awareness. I have a deep and abiding hope for you and for the future of humanity. I already see changes all around us—people waking up to being more loving, more accepting, seeking greater meaning and balance in their lives. As each of us elevates our consciousness, I truly believe, all of humanity changes. My hope is that you will walk this path with the thousands of other people who are living in this inspired and empowered way. May you finally, once and for all, calm the chaos of your life!

References

Anderson, Craig; Gentile, Douglas and Buckley, Katherine. (2007). *Violent Video Games Effect on Children and Adolescents: Theory, Research and Public Policy.* Oxford: Oxford University Press

Ben-Shahar, Tal, Ph.D. (2007). *Happier: Learn the Secrets to Daily Joy and Lasting Fulfillment.* New York: McGraw-Hill.

Braden, Nathaniel. (1969, 2001). *The Psychology of Self Esteem: A Revolutionary Approach to Self Understanding that Launched a New Era in Modern Psychology.* New York: John Wiley & Sons, Inc.

Bushman, Brad and Anderson, Craig. (2007). Comfortably Numb: The desensitizing effects of violent media on helping others, *Association for Psychological Science, 20,* p. 273-277.

Drucker, Peter. (2010). Managing Oneself in *Harvard Business Review's 10 MUST Reads On Managing Yourself.* Boston: Harvard Business School Publishing Corporation.

Falco, Howard. (2014). *Time in a Bottle: Mastering The Experience of Time.* New York: Jeremy P. Tarcher/Penguin Group.

Freston, Kathy. (2009). *Quantum Wellness: A Practical Guide to Health and Happiness.* New York: Weinstein Books.

Hammerness, Paul, M.D., & Margaret Moore (2012). *Organize Your Mind, Organize Your Life: Train Your Brain to Get More Done in Less Time.* Boston: Harvard University.

Hawkins, David, M.D., Ph.D. (2006). *Transcending the Levels of Consciousness: The Stairway to Enlightenment.* West Sedona, Arizona: Veritas Publishing.

Kolbert, Elizabeth. (2014). Why are we so busy? *The New Yorker,* May 26, 2014.

Needleman, Jacob. (2003). *Time and The Soul: Where Has All the Meaningful Time Gone—and Can We Get It Back?* San Francisco: Berrett-Koehler Publishers, Inc.

Orloff Judith, M.D. (2005). *Positive Energy: Ten Extraordinary Prescriptions for Transforming Fatigue, Stress and Fear into Vibrance, Strength and Love.* New York: Harmony Publishers.

Parks, Linda (2013). *Clear Your Space, Clear Your Mind.* Clear Your Space, Inc.

Pert, Candice, Ph.D. (1999). *Molecules of Emotion: The Science Behind Mind-Body Medicine.* New York: Simon and Schuster.

Pert, Candice, Ph.D. (2006). *Everything You Need to Know to Feel Go(o)d.* Australia: Hayhouse Publishing.

Ray, Paul and Sherry Ruth Anderson. (2001). *The Cultural Creatives: How 50 Million People are Changing the World.* New York: Three Rivers Press.

Robbins, John. (2011). *The Food Revolution: How Your Diet Can Help Save Your Life and Our World.* San Francisco: Conari Press.

Schneider, Bruce, Ph.D. (2008). *Energy Leadership: Transforming Your Workplace and Your Life from the Core.* Hoboken, New Jersey: John Wiley & Sons, Inc.

Schwartz, Tony and McCarthy, Catherine. (2010). Manage Your Energy Not Your Time in *Harvard Business Review's 10 MUST Reads On Managing Yourself.* Boston: Harvard Business School Publishing Corporation.

Smith, Hyrum. (1994). *The 10 Natural Laws of Successful Time and Life Management: Proven Strategies for Increased Productivity and Inner Peace.* New York: Warner Books, Inc.

Strom, Max. (2013). *There Is No App for Happiness: How to Avoid a Near-Life Experience.* New York: Skyhorse Publishing.